The Green Eyeshades of War

An Examination of Financial Management during War

by

GEN LARRY O. SPENCER
37TH VICE-CHIEF OF STAFF OF THE AIR FORCE

Air University Press
Curtis E. LeMay Center for Doctrine Development and Education
Maxwell Air Force Base, Alabama

Project Editor
Dr. Ernest Allan Rockwell

Copy Editor
Sandi Davis

Cover Art
L. Susan Fair

Book Design and Illustrations
L. Susan Fair

Composition and Prepress Production
Michele D. Harrell

Print Preparation and Distribution
Diane Clark

AIR UNIVERSITY PRESS

Director and Publisher
Dr. Ernest Allan Rockwell

Deputy Director
Lt Col Todd M. Toman, USAF

Air University Press
600 Chennault Circle Bldg. 1405
Maxwell AFB, AL 36112-6026
http://www.airuniversity.af.mil/AUPress/

Facebook:
https://www.facebook.com/AirUnivPress
and
Twitter: https://www.twitter.com/aupress

AIR UNIVERSITY PRESS

Library of Congress Cataloging-in-Publication Data

Names: Spencer, Larry O., 1953- author.
    Title: The green eyeshades of war: an examination
of financial management during war / by Gen Larry
O. Spencer, 37th Vice-Chief of Staff of the Air Force.
    Other titles: Examination of financial management
during war
    Description: [First edition] | Maxwell Air Force
Base, Alabama: Air University Press, Air Force
Research Institute, [2016]
    Includes bibliographical references and index.
    Identifiers: LCCN 2016014045 | ISBN
9781585662616
    Subjects: LCSH: United States—Armed Forces—
Accounting—Case studies. | World War, 1939-1945—
Finance—United States. | Vietnam War, 1961-1975—
Finance—United States. | Persian Gulf War, 1991—
Finance—United States. | Iraq War, 2003-2011—
Finance—United States.
    Classification: LCC UB163 .S64 2016 | DDC
355.6/220973--dc23

First printing July 2016
Second printing May 2018

Disclaimer

Contents

Illustrations

Figures

About the Author

Gen Larry O. Spencer, USAF, retired from active duty on 1 October 2015 as the 37th vice-chief of staff of the Air Force and with nearly 44 years of active service. He is one of the very few who began as an enlisted Airman and rose to the rank of general. General Spencer is also the first Air Force officer promoted to the four-star rank with a primary specialty of financial management. As such, he is uniquely qualified to discuss financial management issues as they relate to the Department of Defense. In particular, his financial experience includes extensive support of two major war operations. As the wing comptroller for the 4th Fighter Wing at Seymour Johnson AFB, North Carolina, then-Major Spencer supported Operations Desert Shield and Desert Storm. Based in large part on his support of the war, Major Spencer's squadron was named "Best in the Air Force" for two consecutive years—an accomplishment that has never been matched. Major Spencer was also named the "Best Comptroller" in the Air Force. Additionally, during an important inspection just after the war, his squadron was rated "outstanding . . . best seen to date." As the command comptroller for Air Combat Command at Langley AFB, Virginia, then-Colonel Spencer oversaw financial operations for Operations Enduring Freedom and Iraqi Freedom. For his support of war operations, he was named "Best Major Command Comptroller in the Department of Defense." General Spencer is currently president of the Air Force Association (AFA). In that capacity, in addition to leading the AFA professional staff, he heads the AFA Veterans Benefit Association and the Air Force Memorial Foundation and serves as publisher of the monthly *Air Force Magazine*.

Acknowledgments

I acknowledge my wife for her support and indulgence for the hours I devoted to writing and researching materials for this work. I offer thanks to all of those who contributed their personal accounts of financial management during war. I also acknowledge the staff of Air University Press for their expertise and guidance. I particularly thank Dr. Ernest Allan Rockwell for his editing support and advice. I thank the hundreds of financial managers that served heroically during war despite the obvious deficits in training and materials. In particular, I thank the men and women who served with me in the 4th Comptroller Squadron at Seymour Johnson AFB, North Carolina, during Operations Desert Shield/Storm and those assigned to the Air Combat Command comptroller staff during Operations Enduring Freedom and Iraqi Freedom. I will forever be grateful for your service and friendship. Finally, I thank God for his enduring support and protection of my family and me.

Introduction

In 415 BC, during a speech to his people, the Syracusan general Hermocrates said, "[The Athenians] have abundance of gold and silver, and these make war, like other things, go smoothly."[1] The presumption that wealthy countries will generally be victorious in battle against adversaries with limited resources is embedded in that statement. Given inflationary factors since 415 BC, I wonder if the sheer magnitude of the costs of war in the twenty-first century would cause even Hermocrates pause.

Roman author, orator, and politician Cicero said, "Endless money forms the sinews of war."[2] In 1499 Gian Giacomo Trivulzio, who held several military commands during the Italian wars, told King Louis XII of France, "To carry on war, three things are necessary: money, money, and yet more money."[3] Finally, in the American War of Independence, Nathanael Greene said, "Without a military chest, it is next to impossible to employ an army with effect."[4] There is a subtle presumption buried in these quotations that is unspoken but nonetheless true in war: the presumption that states with wealth have the capacity and training necessary to manage those large sums of money during war. The Golden Rule states, "He who has the gold, makes the rules." What is missing from that axiom is the assumption that "he who has the gold knows how to manage the gold."

The US history of money and war is indeed a storied one, filled with struggles and a lack of preparedness on the battlefield. From its earliest history, the Second Continental Congress named James Warren the first paymaster general in July 1775. Despite having the term "general" in his title, he was actually a civilian. Warren was essentially in charge of the finances of the Continental Army under George Washington. Once the war started, paymasters appointed from the regiments and battalions within the Continental Army struggled mightily because they had to learn their trade on the job.[5]

In the period around the Mexican–American War (1846–48), much of the country operated using regional currency. This situation meant that states or smaller regions issued their own currency, which was not necessarily recognized by neighboring states. As a result, the federal government paid soldiers with hard currency—actual coins containing gold or silver—but executing those payments proved cumbersome at best to transport or carry. According to Robert McConnell, curator of the Finance Corps Museum at Fort Jackson, South Carolina,

"Pay during World War I did not go smoothly." To help the struggling pay clerks, they were all temporarily promoted to second lieutenants just to minimize the chance of their being "shanghaied."[6]

The United States is blessed with an abundance of resources. As such, the amount of money consumed during wartime has been substantial. However, the US military's ability to manage those large sums of money is another matter. A 7 September 2003 *USA Today* article noted that "the monthly bill for U.S. military missions in Iraq and Afghanistan now rivals Pentagon spending during the Vietnam War. . . . The Pentagon is spending nearly $5 billion per month in Iraq and Afghanistan."[7] Therefore, from the outset of the Iraq and Afghanistan wars, it was clear that the United States possessed an abundance of resources.

However, when a 2002 General Accounting Office (GAO) report found that as much as $101 million in contingency operations funds were spent on questionable expenditures, the US government's ability to manage those funds was called into question.[8] That same report concluded that limited guidance and oversight, combined with a lack of cost consciousness, were significant contributors to the problem. The GAO surmised that unless the Department of Defense (DOD) developed more definitive guidance and increased oversight, the problems of managing funds during contingency operations would likely continue.[9]

This brings into focus an important question. If we recognize that success in war requires large sums of money and resources, is our military prepared to manage those funds during war? This question sets the stage for the following chapters that will walk through the history of money and war to determine how effectively the military has managed money during times of conflict.

The reason for addressing this issue is simple yet critical. In today's environment, the efficient and effective use of taxpayer dollars is paramount to congressional and public support. Without that support, as Hermocrates observed, US involvement in war might not go smoothly. However, even as the United States defeated the Iraqi regime and embarked on rebuilding efforts, the debate over the military's management of money during war continued.

As the initial stages of Operation Iraqi Freedom concluded, congressional leaders were at odds with the White House over the costs. Cong. Earl Pomeroy (D-ND), who visited Iraq, said, "The rebuilding of Iraq will be significantly more expensive, more dangerous and take longer than the American people have been prepared for."[10] In addition, Cong. Jim Nussle (R-IA), chairman, House Budget Committee, planned to expediently call DOD officials for hearings in front of his committee to get more detailed accounting of the costs of Iraq's reconstruction and occupation.[11]

Today there are threats of war and violence at every turn. Even in the middle of the debate over Gulf War spending, US naval ships were poised off the coast of Liberia in anticipation of possible US intervention. In North Korea, Russia, Syria, Iran, areas controlled by the Islamic State, and elsewhere, the potential for conflict in the future is as evident as it is complicated. Lone-wolf terrorist attacks, cyber threats, and vulnerabilities in space that were far-fetched in the minds of our predecessors are very real today.

I frame this picture of current and future threats to the United States only to add credence and credibility to why an examination of war and money is critically important. If I could modify the words of Hermocrates to fit the twenty-first century, I would say that sufficient amounts and the *efficient management* of money are critical elements necessary to make war go smoothly.

Some might wonder why money and war are so inextricably linked. The United States is a nation with a $17 trillion gross domestic product.[12] Couple that fact with the strongest, most-feared military in the world and most observers would conclude that victory in battle is all but a foregone conclusion, given our vast war chest. However, an examination of our financial history in war might suggest otherwise. Spending during World War II was characterized as an open checkbook. However, today Congress and the American public demand full accounting of taxpayer dollars—even during war.

Additionally, commanders can ill afford the distraction of poor financial management on the battlefield. The "shock and awe" of Operation Iraqi Freedom clearly demonstrated the sophistication and synchronization of modern joint warfare. Can one imagine a deployed commander huddled around the war-planning table agonizing over every minute detail of an attack only to be interrupted with pay problems or to be told that a critical piece of war equipment was not approved in the budget?

Does this sound far-fetched? Consider an incident during Operation Urgent Fury in Grenada, roughly 10 years after the Vietnam War. In his autobiography *It Doesn't Take a Hero*, Gen H. Norman Schwarzkopf described an extremely chaotic scene involving ranger attacks and helicopter support under extreme combative stress during the operation. In the middle of the turmoil, the admiral in charge of operations received an urgent message from the office of the Navy's comptroller in Washington, DC, warning that the admiral should not refuel Army helicopters until the funds-transfer arrangements had been finalized between the Army and Navy![13]

Another point to consider in evaluating the worth of such an examination of wartime financial performance is the ever-increasing technology of modern warfare. Anyone that witnessed the precision of US war-fighting capability during Operation Desert Storm most assuredly came away impressed with our technological advantage. However, behind every quantum leap in military capability was a concurrent leap in costs to research, develop, procure, field, and sustain those systems. Also, consider that we are in the middle of a changing pattern of history. When the Soviet Union dissolved, the United States assumed political and military predominance in the world. The price we pay for that preeminence is the fact that US forces are increasingly sought after to resolve regional conflicts and preserve the peace. Shifting priorities in the United States further complicate this changing pattern.

An increasing budget deficit, an unstable economy, demands for better education and health-care reform, and calls to reform entitlement programs are but a few of the major problems competing for scarce domestic attention and resources. Thus, to state the obvious, the DOD can ill afford to mismanage money during any period— particularly during conflict, when the financial costs are so high.

In this evolving world environment that many believe will spawn more frequent and increasingly expensive military operations, I predict that the battle cry will not be victory at any cost, as it was in World War II. To the contrary, this new world order will demand victory at the most efficient and most economical cost. In this new world order, full financial support for contingencies is not a given. In fact, getting the funds necessary to win our nation's wars depends upon our military having the confidence of Congress and the American people that military financial managers can and will effectively and efficiently execute those funds during times of conflict. The question is, are we up to the task?

This monograph will put military financial management during war on trial, examining fiscal performance and readiness during various conflicts: World War II, Vietnam, Operations Desert Shield/Storm, and Operations Enduring Freedom/Iraqi Freedom. Each of these conflicts is unique, yet each situation validated the critical need for sound fiscal management and controls. Let the trial begin.

Notes

1. Benjamin Jowett, *Thucydides*, 2nd ed. (Oxford, UK: Oxford University Press, 1900), 205.

2. Quoted in Robert W. Kolb, ed., *Sovereign Debt: From Safety to Default* (Hoboken, NJ: John Wiley & Sons, 2011), 1.

3. Quoted in Robert Debs Heinl Jr., ed., *Dictionary of Military and Naval Quotations* (Annapolis, MD: Naval Institute Press, 1966), 115.

4. Quoted in Lee Patrick Anderson, *The Life & Times of Major-General Nathanael Greene* (Boca Raton, FL: Universal Publishers, 2002), 242.

5. Clifford Kyle Jones, "Finance Corps Has History of Meeting Challenges," *NCO Journal*, 9 July 2013, http://ncojournal.dodlive.mil/2013/07/09/finance-corps-has -history-of-meeting-challenges/.

6. Quoted in ibid.

7. Dave Moniz, "Monthly Costs of Iraq, Afghan Wars Approach That of Vietnam," *USA Today*, 7 September 2003, http://usatoday30.usatoday.com/news/world/iraq/2003 -09-07-cover-costs_x.htm.

8. General Accounting Office (GAO), *Defense Budget: Need to Strengthen Guidance and Oversight of Contingency Operations Costs* (Washington, DC: GAO, May 2002), 2, http://www.gao.gov/new.items/d02450.pdf. The GAO was renamed the Government Accountability Office in 2004.

9. Ibid., 3.

10. Moniz, "Monthly Costs."

11. Ibid.

12. World Bank, "GDP (current US$)," 10 April 2015, http://data.worldbank.org /indicator/NY.GDP.MKTP.CD.

13. H. Norman Schwarzkopf and Peter Petre, *It Doesn't Take a Hero* (New York: Bantam, 2010), 250.

Chapter 1

World War II

Setting the Stage

The Open Checkbook

To win World War II, the United States consumed $176 billion—a sum that still staggers the imagination, even considering the immense inflation subsequent to 1945.[1] Although that large expenditure of dollars helped achieve a decisive US victory, the fiscal management of those dollars was anything but decisive. In fact, many people considered financial stewardship during World War II downright disgraceful!

The summation of military financial performance during the war is indeed disappointing. Uniformed financial managers were both untrained and unprepared. Walter Rundell, Jr., one of the few authors to focus on military fiscal performance during the war, surmised in his book *Military Money* that "finance officers were forced to cope with wartime financing as best they could, by improvising and muddling through."[2] The military financial community was so unprepared for the war that the first finance unit did not arrive in Europe until 26 January 1942. Further, not only did they arrive technically unprepared for wartime operations but also rudimentary financial equipment was missing. "Had no office equipment—just one typewriter and one portable adding machine, which was lost somewhere in shipment, no idea what happened to it," commented an officer in the unit.[3]

Since little thought had been devoted to managing money during war, even the regulations and pay tables were left behind. In fact, as far-fetched as it sounds, the first two months' payrolls had to be computed from memory.[4] Thus, from the onset, military fiscal leaders were late to the fight, untrained to operate under wartime conditions, and lacking the appropriate equipment and documentation for fiscal guidance.

One explanation of why the Finance Department devoted so little effort to war planning was the faulty assumption that peacetime doctrine and systems could easily transition to the battlefield. According to Rundell, "By far the most telling complaint registered against the pay system overseas was its design for peacetime operations. Before the war began, those in the Finance Department responsible for planning had failed to foresee that the existing method of payment was not fitted for overseas."[5]

Stateside payments to troops were relatively easy because it was simple to muster them in a group for an orderly process. However, during the war, finance agents had to "chase around all over the countryside looking for their men when they should have been free to command them in the field. That the job got done over there was a credit to the men running the system, not to the system itself."[6]

The impact of not planning financially for the war manifested itself in a host of problems and miscues, including the nonpayment of troops in the field. Units assigned to the Aleutian Islands and the Hawaii Department, at one point, were actually not paid for six and four months, respectively.[7] The nonpayment issue reached such proportions throughout the theater that Gen George C. Marshall was compelled to notify all theater commanders about the extent of the problems. In an official notification, General Marshall not only complained about delayed payments in-theater but also lamented that many returnees to the States had not been paid in months. Marshall further encouraged all theater commanders to give special attention to correcting pay problems.[8]

To compensate for inadequacies in troop pay, "partial" or "advance" payments were often issued to cover incidental expenses. However, since there was no plan to account for such payments, abuse frequently resulted—particularly for the Army Air Corps. Since flying duties resulted in frequent movement, individuals would continue to draw advance payments as they moved from one location to another even though the additional payments were not authorized. Unfortunately, since the Finance Department had no system of verification, there was virtually no way of detecting the unauthorized payments.[9]

Aside from deficiencies in troop payments, local vendor and contractual support, an often-overlooked task of military financial managers during war, was also problematic. During the war, US forces contracted with local vendors for such critical wartime support as aircraft maintenance and logistical support. The problem was that payments for these services in an overseas wartime environment bore little resemblance to those in peacetime operations.

For example, areas like northern Australia, which continued to embrace the bartering concept, demanded payment in beads, mirrors, colorful cloth, and cosmetics instead of currency.[10] Illiterate Bedouins in Morocco used thumbprints to verify identification rather than the signatory process used in the United States.[11] These methods of payment and currency verification may seem ancient now; however, when you consider the criticality of the goods and services being purchased, this shortcoming was indeed a major one in supporting war operations.

The Finance Department also should have recognized that the deployment of massive numbers of US troops abroad would lead to the financial requirement to apportion pay due to dependents in the form of military allotments. With that recognition, the Finance Department could have worked with the Office of Dependency Benefits, the central Department of War agency for mailing allotment checks, to ensure the smooth implementation of payments to family members back home.

However, such recognition was not forthcoming. Sloppy and cumbersome procedures led Brig Gen L. S. Ostrander, adjutant general for United States Army Forces in the Far East (USAFFE), to comment that this financial mismanagement created "a serious morale lapse" in his theater.[12] In late 1943 between 4,000 and 6,000 allotment payments were 6–12 months behind schedule. The chief finance officer of the Southwest Pacific area (SWPA) protested, "I realize the Office of Dependency Benefits has its problems, but when those problems become a year old, it's very hard to explain . . . to troops in the combat area."[13]

Yet another miscue in fiscal management involved foreign currency exchanges. In terms of preparedness for war, the fact that the Department of War's Office of the Fiscal Director in Washington did not distribute a foreign exchange guide to the field until September 1943—nearly two years after the war began—clearly indicates little forethought concerning financial management in a war zone. Prior to the issuance of the guide, currency exchange procedures were piecemeal and did not reflect consistent fiscal policy.[14]

The impact of an inconsistent currency exchange policy was outright fraud and a thriving black market. For example, the Persian Gulf Command (PGC) was particularly vulnerable to currency exchange tampering. Iran was the hub that controlled large quantities of marketable commodities destined for the Soviet Union through the US lend-lease program. Since there were few controls on foreign currency, lend-lease goods were often sold on the black market at considerable profit. Since there were no restrictions on the amount of currency converted back to US dollars, departing merchant seamen became particularly adept at this illegal yet highly profitable venture.

The PGC finally developed a control mechanism that clamped down on this profiteering scheme in 1945.[15] Sadly, this development may have been a case of too little too late because this type of activity had gone essentially unchecked for nearly four years.

An even more alarming case of fraudulent activity actually involved a military finance cashier. The sergeant's scheme was not a complicated one. He simply set up the unit's bank account in his own name and then purchased a large number of French francs and Italian lire with Egyptian pounds at rates below the legal rate of exchange. Next, he reversed the transactions by exchanging his francs and lire for Egyptian pounds at the higher official rate. Fortunately, the cashier was discovered and subsequently court-martialed.[16] Nevertheless, these examples of poor fiscal controls clearly show that military financial managers were not prepared to go to war.

During World War II, senior commanders placed great pressure on financial managers to do things that were either inappropriate or illegal. A captain disbursing officer assigned to the Finance Office in Melbourne, Australia, refused commercial payments to local nationals because the payments exceeded his authorization. Gen Douglas MacArthur objected and wanted the payments to be promptly made. To the disbursing agent's credit as the accountable official, he told General MacArthur he was legally required to follow the fiscal laws and regulations and would be held personally liable. Despite the protest, General MacArthur issued the captain a written authorization to make the payments. In 1944 the General Accounting Office (GAO) audited the unauthorized payments and held the captain accountable for $3,368,000. After reviewing General MacArthur's authorization, the GAO acquiesced; however, final relief for the debt came only after congressional legislation.[17]

In hindsight, one might ask the question, Why was the Finance Department given such huge sums of money since the financial community was obviously not prepared to support the war effectively? A close reading of the history provides clear focus to what was an apparent serious lapse in judgment. In stark contrast to anything this country had witnessed before, the emotion surrounding the attack on Pearl Harbor was unprecedented. As a result, despite some early reservations about the Department of War's ability to manage such large sums of money, Congress provided all the funds necessary, an open checkbook if you will, to ensure the total defeat of the once-great Axis powers. Put another way, defeating the enemy meant everything; how we achieved the victory and at what cost were secondary.

To illustrate this state of emotion, the following comments in the congressional record by Cong. D. Lane Powers (R-NJ) of the House Subcommittee on Military Appropriations typify the mood of Congress in 1943 regarding funding for the war:

> It is hard for me and it is hard for anyone else to conceive of $72,000,000,000. In my wildest dreams I just cannot think of that much money. . . . I am frank to admit that there are many items in the $72,000,000,000 that I definitely do not know all about, but I am willing to take the word of our General Staff, and when they tell me that these moneys are needed to promote the war successfully, I say that . . . the money should be granted. . . . I am taking the word of the General Staff of the War Department, people who are running this show. If they tell me this is what they need for the successful prosecution of this war and for ultimate victory, I am for it. Whether it staggers me according to its proportions or not, I am still for it.[18]

Despite the issues of financial unpreparedness, there was a silver lining to this cloud that was to become a trend for all the wars that followed—that is, great people doing great things despite poor training. Rundell recounts the story of one conscientious disbursing officer who unintentionally miscounted payments for 500 enlisted replacements during the Normandy invasion. In his haste to get the troops paid, he had mistaken 500-franc notes for 50-franc notes. Distraught over the miscalculations and perhaps concerned over his personal liability of a loss that totaled 450,000 francs, he grabbed his payroll data and boarded ship, just as the gangplank was being raised. During the journey, he frantically recalculated each payment and balanced out his account as the ship reached shore. Relieved that all was in good order, his thoughts immediately turned toward two questions: how would he get back to England and how could he convince his superiors that he had not gone AWOL.[19]

Postwar Actions

Following the war, a congressional committee reviewing the military's performance reported "unconscionable wastes of money" caused primarily through two shortcomings: the Department of War's failure to adopt modern financial business practices and the lack of a battlefield financial system to accurately record expenditures.[20] Concerned over the findings in the congressional report, the secretary of war directed a separate study of the "business practices" during the war. The final report concluded that no one, from the secretary of war on down, knew the real costs of operations for which they were responsible.[21] In other words, Congress had indeed provided an open checkbook, with little accountability for expenditures. The military consumed $176 billion of taxpayer money during the war, but no one knew exactly where and how the money had been spent.

As a result of these studies, a decision was made after the war to appoint a single individual—experienced in accounting and budgeting—to organize and manage military financial procedures. The new position was intended to parallel that of a comptroller in private industry. Therefore, based on the precedent set by the Air Force that had already achieved great success with the appointment of an Air Force comptroller, the Army established a comptroller position to bring sound fiscal management practices to the Army.[22]

Missing the Mark

The bottom-line verdict in financial management during World War II was that the military financial community was unprepared. This deficiency led to the mismanagement of fiscal resources throughout the war, described in 1943 by Sen. Harry F. Byrd, Sr. (D-VA), chairman of the Joint Committee on Reduction of Nonessential Federal Expenditures, as "unnecessarily extravagant and wasteful."[23] Horror stories, including the nonpayment of entire units for periods up to six months, diverted the attention of senior field commanders and compromised troop morale.

Even seemingly insignificant financial transactions such as partial payments and foreign currency exchanges lacked fiscal controls and led to abuse. In fact, shortcomings with troop pay and currency exchanges resulted in an overdraft of $530,775,440.[24] Commercial vendor and local labor payments proved themselves critical to the warfighting effort. Yet, this important task received little if any preplanning before the war.

The open-checkbook approach to funding eased the burden of accountability in the field. However, this lax means of funding accountability, albeit unintentional, created an environment of waste and uncontrolled spending. As a result, congressional leaders approved—with little insight or validation of the real requirements—huge sums for the war. Also, the general mismanagement of foreign currency throughout the war theater led to fraud and black market ventures.

Finally, despite the myriad of associated financial problems, a combination of the abundance of money provided by Congress, extraordinary efforts on the part of military financial managers, and overwhelming public support for the war clearly overshadowed the poor financial preparedness. Those responsible for wartime financial management had little to fear because no matter how ineffective they were, the money just simply kept coming—backed up by an emotion-laced public.

Nevertheless, World War II established an undeniable necessity in war: not only is the abundance of money critical to winning conflicts but accountability and effective management of money are just as important. Commanders in the field depend heavily on contractual services and efficient troop payments. Congress depends on the military to provide valid cost estimates and to efficiently manage the funds provided to execute the war. Unfortunately, during World War II, the Finance Department fell short on both accounts.

With the war concluded, the task and challenge for military financial managers were to eliminate the mistakes of the past and prepare for the future. However, if in fact the Finance Department accepted the challenge, it fell short of the goal since its initial performance during the war in Vietnam showed very little—if any—improvement.

Notes

1. Walter Rundell, Jr., *Military Money: A Fiscal History of the U.S. Army Overseas in World War II* (College Station: Texas A&M University Press, 1980), xii.

2. Ibid., 4.

3. Personal letter from Capt Clarence Neely, identified by Col Louis A. Hawkins. Cited in ibid., 37.

4. Rundell, *Military Money*, 37.

5. Ibid., 142.

6. Interview with Col Grester, 30 March 1954. Cited in ibid., 143.

7. "Historical Report, Detachment Finance Section, Alaska Department"; Col R. E. Fraile, adjutant general, Hawaiian Dept., to Distribution D, letter, subject: Prompt Payment of Troops, FIN 241, 22 July 1943; and Record Group 338. Cited in Rundell, *Military Money*, 143.

8. Marshall to HQ USAFIME, AMSME, no. 6233, 12 August 43. Record Group 338. Cited in Rundell, *Military Money*, 143.

9. Rundell, *Military Money*, 148–49.

10. Military Intelligence Section, Far East Command, *History of the United States Army Forces in the Far East, 1943–1945* (Manila, Philippines: US Army, 1974), 99.

11. Col Oliver Williams de Gruchy, chief, Fiscal Branch, HQ Persian Gulf Command (PGC), to command signal officer, PGSC, memorandum, 18 January 1943.

12. Brig Gen L. S. Ostrander, adjutant general, USAFFE, to TAG, letter, subject: Discontinuance of Class E Allotments, 6 September 1943.

13. Col L. W. Maddox, chief financial officer, SWPA, to FIS DIR, ASF, letter, subject: Progress Report of Fiscal and Finance Activities in SWPA, 8 December 1943.

14. Rundell, *Military Money*, 207.

15. Ibid., 214.

16. Col R. E. Odell, fiscal director, HQ United States Army Forces in the Middle East (USAFIME), for CG, USAFIME, memorandum, subject: Report of Operations, 22 December 44.

17. Rundell, *Military Money*, 53–54.

18. House, *Congressional Record* 89, 78th Cong., 1st sess., 19 June 1943, 6155–56.

19. Alfred A. Abbott, "The Army as Banker," *Army Information Digest* 2, no. 8 (August 1947): 37, http://babel.hathitrust.org/cgi/pt?id=mdp.39015082112494;view =1up;seq=985.

20. Harry M. DeWitt, *Comptrollership in the Armed Forces: A Summary and Comparative Evaluation of Comptrollership in Industry and the Department of Defense with Special Reference to Program Management and Management Engineering As Included in the Functions of the Army Comptroller* (Washington, DC: Institute of Engineering, 1952), 21.

21. James E. Hewes, *From Root to McNamara: Army Organization and Administration, 1900–1963* (Washington, DC: Center of Military History, 1975), 179.

22. Louis C. Seelig, *Resource Management in Peace and War* (Washington, DC: National Defense University Press, 1990), 23.

23. House, *Congressional Record* 89, 6707.

24. Walter Rundell, *Black Market Money: Collapse of U.S. Military Currency Control in World War II* (Baton Rouge: Louisiana State University Press, 1964), 245.

Chapter 2

Vietnam

Repeating Past Mistakes

*By the late 1960s . . . public support for the Vietnam War began
to dissolve. Reflecting the division among the citizens, Congress
began using its chief power beyond lawmaking—the power of
the purse strings—to control the operation of the war.*

—Louis C. Seelig

Resource Management in Peace and War

Different Folks, Same Strokes!

From a financial perspective, the early days of Vietnam were eerily
similar to World War II. During March 1965, Secretary of Defense
Robert McNamara (see fig. 1) promised the service secretaries "an
unlimited appropriation" to fund operations in Vietnam. He subsequently informed the joint chiefs that they should not "feel any con-
straints whatsoever—absolutely none."[1] Based on the joint chiefs'
experience in funding previous conflicts, they concluded that the
secretary had handed them a blank check.

This sentiment also carried over to Congress and the White House.
The 1965 emergency supplemental funding request overwhelmingly
passed in the House and the Senate. The day after budget approval,
Pres. Lyndon Johnson called a press conference and associated the
speedy congressional approval with American public support to engage in Vietnam. President Johnson informed reporters that US
troops had a "blank check" as assurance of full national support.[2]

In an interesting twist, despite previous pronouncements alluding
to unlimited spending, Secretary McNamara insisted that the war be
conducted as cost efficiently as possible. McNamara's cost-reduction
strategy involved three facets: (1) buying only what was needed; (2)
buying at the lowest sound price; and (3) reducing operating costs
through integration and standardization.[3] Despite McNamara's good
intentions, these efforts backfired because the policy of "buying only

what we need" resulted in significant shortfalls on the battlefield, particularly when unanticipated escalations in operations occurred.[4]

Figure 1. Secretary of Defense Robert McNamara briefing the press on events in Vietnam. (Photograph VA002823, 26 April 1965, Douglas Pike Photograph Collection, The Vietnam Center and Archive, Texas Tech University, http://www.vietnam.ttu.edu/virtualarchive/items.php?item=VA 002823.)

Escalations were particularly problematic for the Air Force because the demand for bombs and rockets quickly exceeded the supply. These critical shortfalls reached the point in 1966 where McNamara was forced to ask Congress to reprogram funds to purchase 196 additional fighter-bombers.[5] Reported shortfalls on the battlefield caused scathing attacks on the secretary of defense. In July 1965 Rep. L. Mendel Rivers (D-SC), chairman of the House Committee on Armed Services, requested that Rep. Porter Hardy Jr. (D-VA), chairman of the Special Investigations Subcommittee, Committee on Armed Services, "conduct an immediate inquiry" into the secretary of defense's reduction programs.[6]

Congressman Hardy's subcommittee issued a classified report identifying shortages in ammunition, rockets, flares, missiles, and

500- and 750-pound bombs that directly hampered combat operations. Committee members focused on the worldwide shortage of spare parts, blaming those shortages on McNamara's "apparent overzealous dedication to economy" at the expense of combat troops.[7] Thus, for a brief period, it appeared that McNamara might change the course of financial management history that featured large sums of money to manage on the battlefield. However, the financial history of Vietnam would remain unchanged from that of past conflicts.

With McNamara's cost-efficiency efforts brushed aside, expanded forces, enormous defense budgets, and bloated supplemental requests replaced economy and lower defense budgets. The war forced McNamara to increase conventional military strength far in excess of any strategic plan, much less his own. Compelled to bow to political pressure, he saw military manpower rise roughly 20 percent, from 2.85 million in 1965 to 3.4 million in 1968.[8]

With these increases, the financial pendulum of the Vietnam War swung from one end to the other and then back again, but it would change even once more. Initially, both the secretary of defense and the president assured military leaders that, when it came to financing the war, their budget cup would run over—just as it had in the past. Upon reflection, the secretary of defense, who detested excess spending, reversed course and insisted that those funds be tightly managed and that war spending be heavily scrutinized. In the end, rather than self-correct to a position between the two extremes, the secretary overreached, resulting in shortfalls in critical equipment and supplies on the battlefield. This situation caused the pendulum to swing back full circle to the "open checkbook" side of the financial spectrum. Thus, financial managers in Vietnam were once again faced with managing large sums of money on the battlefield. And still, they were neither trained nor prepared to do so.

As Leonard B. Taylor states, "To military financial managers . . . Vietnam was a nightmare. It was much like starting out a game of baseball with the normal rules and during the third inning, finding out that you were playing basketball."[9] With roughly 20 years to build upon the experiences of World War II, it was as though a time warp had wiped away those years. As they had in World War II, financial managers entered the war assuming that the peacetime rules would be sufficient; however, much to their dismay, they were playing the wrong game. Poor financial practices were more easily accepted during

World War II because it was total war—do or die—and the entire country was behind it.

Vietnam was a strikingly different conflict than its immediate predecessors. It was a limited war, fought in a single theater, and although initial public support was strong, as the war dragged on, public support soured. Moreover, the combination of declining public support for the war (for example, see fig. 2) and the Department of Defense's (DOD) inability to manage large sums of money in Vietnam once again caused the financial pendulum to overcorrect. With Congress inserting itself to pull back on the financial reins, this financial pendular dynamic only exacerbated the problems of financial management during the war.

Figure 2. Veterans for Peace at the March on the Pentagon, 21 October 1967. (National Archives Identifier: 2803434, Local Identifier: 7049-30, Series: Johnson White House Photographs, 11 11/22 22/1963 1963 - 1 1/20 20/1969, 1969 Collection LBJ-WHPO: White House Photo Office Collection.)

As was the case in World War II, lack of accountability was the financial Achilles' heel of Vietnam. In short, between 1965 and 1975, the United States spent $111 billion for the Vietnam War ($836 billion in 2015 dollars), but military financial managers were not prepared to track those expenditures.[10] A significant roadblock that contributed to the problem was a policy decision to keep administrative duties and personnel to a minimum in-theater.

This policy to reduce combat service-support units resulted in a dichotomy for the financial management community. The war demanded a heavy reliance on contract support from local Vietnamese vendors, third-country firms, and continental US organizations.[11] However, since the DOD had not planned for limited financial personnel in-theater, there was no plan to compensate for the personnel reduction. This shortsightedness led to continued frustration over the lack of accountability—to the point where the early 1970s showed a marked turn in the relationship between the DOD and Congress. Having completely lost confidence in the DOD's ability to account for expenditures, Congress exerted its power of the purse to send a clear message to the department: *no more blank check.*

A memorandum issued by Headquarters Military Assistance Command, Vietnam (MACV) to all field commanders illustrates that the message was received loud and clear: "During fiscal year 1970 there has been increasing pressure to reduce spending within DOD. This has been evidenced by the receipt of actual funding authorizations that are far below previously budgeted requirements. From all indications to date, the austere funding limitations will continue for the next several years. Accordingly, efforts must be initiated now to effect substantial reductions in all elements of cost and to initiate a program that will insure the conservation not just of funds, but all other MACV resources as well."[12]

This inability of the DOD to properly account for funds during the war drove a financial wedge of distrust between Congress and the department. Perhaps it was the open-checkbook policies of the past that caused the DOD to adopt an attitude of indifference toward financial management and war. Either way, Vietnam demonstrated that Congress can and will use its fiscal leverage to influence actions on the battlefield. If the DOD cannot manage money properly during war, Congress will either manage that money for the department or withdraw financial support.

An example of financial ineptitude during Vietnam was the management of reimbursements. Typically, a reimbursement occurs when one agency provides a service to another and is paid for that service. In the case of Vietnam, if the Air Force, for example, provided a service to the Army (financially smart because this practice saves duplication and overhead costs), the Army would reimburse the Air Force for that service through a billing process. In Vietnam the combination of the limited administrative personnel policy and no effective wartime accounting system strangled the reimbursement program at its very core.

The issue of reimbursements was particularly chronic between the Air Force and the Army. In "Loss of Army Resources in Support of Reimbursable Customers," a personal memorandum on the subject, Gen Dwight E. Beach, commanding general of US Army Pacific, stated, "This problem is a matter of command concern at all levels. It is apparent that more positive action is required to safeguard against the issue of resources without reimbursement. The administrative workload involved in documenting issues to reimbursable customers cannot justify the Army's failure to obtain proper documentation to support billings. This is another task that must be accomplished. In the future, support should not be furnished to reimbursable customers unless they present the required documentation."[13] A June 1967 message from the Department of the Army to US Army, Pacific, warned of an "unwarranted deficiency" and an "unexplainable and embarrassing" situation.[14]

Following an audit that confirmed severe problems managing reimbursements, a full-spectrum review was conducted to strengthen financial management systems operating in the Pacific. The review uncovered examples such as a $200,000-per-month subsistence to the Air Force that had not been billed in over two years. Another involved storage, distribution, and transportation of bulk petroleum between the Army and the Air Force, whereby no documentation was maintained for two years.[15] Again, the root cause can be traced to inadequate financial policies and systems in the theater.

In September 1962 Capt Charlie Metcalf, who would later retire as a major general, became the first Air Force accounting and finance officer assigned in the Republic of Vietnam. He activated that country's first military finance office at Tan Son Nhut Air Base.[16] Before Metcalf established a finance office, he was a paying agent attached to Clark Air Base, Philippines. Since the Air Force operated on a strictly cash basis in those days, he literally had to travel throughout South Vietnam making cash payments to Air Force members in the field.[17]

While establishing his new in-country finance operation, all Captain Metcalf had was a two-drawer safe inside a hut with a thatch roof. At the time, his top concern was the fact that he literally had to "wing it" in terms of procedures and fiscal guidance. He lamented that there were no established guidelines to operate in a war theater, and he and his small staff of five had to write their own procedures as they went along.[18]

Captain Metcalf related a story involving a loss of funds that he will never forget. He was directed to send $25,000 in cash to a paying agent at a forward location for payday. To do so, he put the $25,000 in a canvas bag and placed it on a helicopter for transport forward. Unfortunately, during the flight, the helicopter crashed into a rice patty field. War zone or not, a significant loss of funds is a serious matter—one that weighed heavily on his mind. However, much to his relief, about two weeks later, a gruff looking Army noncommissioned officer showed up at his hut and threw a thoroughly drenched canvas bag containing exactly $25,000 in very damp bills on his desk.[19]

In 1967 Air Force lieutenant Jan W. Brassem, acting comptroller at Pleiku Air Base, South Vietnam, found that payments for local contractor support were nothing like those for which stateside training prepared him. Since local vendors could not come on base, he had to travel to the vendors' residences for payment. Brassem stated, "There is no rush to collect payment. No rush to do more business. There is none of the normal business practices, but rather a few cups of tea, some light conversation (due to the language barrier), and finally the cash payment."[20]

Similarly, support of regulatory and physical infrastructure, albeit in a war zone, was far less than that required for sound financial operations. When Lieutenant Brassem first arrived in November 1966, the finance office was a building with cardboard walls and minimal security. As he recalled, "Anyone could put his foot through the cashier's cage and have access to all the safes." This concern led to the posting of a guard 24 hours a day. Also, current manuals and regulations were "rare" and often "scrounged" from stateside bases.[21]

The Silver Lining: Military Pay

The first thing a man does when he arrives in Southeast Asia is mark his calendar to show the date of his return to the States. Next he looks for mail from home. Then he thinks about pay.

—Jan W. Brassem

"The 'Money' Man in Vietnam"

The payment of troops in the field, although difficult, was largely a good news story. However, it must be noted that Vietnam marked the beginning of a striking contrast in US war fighting as it relates to military pay: the one-year tour. This situation meant that troops generally served in the war zone for only one year rather than fighting for the duration, as had been the case in earlier conflicts.

Figure 3. Col J. L. "Jumbo" Evans, Lt Col Sara N. Harris, Capt Cynthia Little, Col Farley E. Peebles, Maj Ralph Law, and Lt Col John Fippen all holding letters from the governor of the state of Alabama. (Photograph VA061712, n.d., Farley E. Peebles Collection, The Vietnam Center and Archive, Texas Tech University, http://www.vietnam.ttu.edu/virtualar chive/items.php?item=VA061712.)

Vietnam was also unique in that it was tactically fought using largely a "base camp" strategy, meaning that troops would deploy to the field for specific missions and subsequently return to their base camp. Since most base camps were located near South Vietnamese towns and contained the full complement of exchange services and club facilities, payday was a popular time of the month. The significance of this evolutionary change was that it placed a heightened importance on commanders to ensure timely and accurate payment of the troops in the field.

As an example of just how popular payday was, Air Force lieutenant colonel John Fippen (see fig. 3), base comptroller at Ton San Nhut Air Base, South Vietnam, described the financial picture immediately following the Tet Offensive of 31 January 1968—a major North Vietnamese and Vietcong attack on American, South Vietnamese, and allied forces—as any other military payday, just busier.[22] Despite a major enemy offensive of 70,000 troops, once the primary fighting subsided, the immediate concern of the troops in the field was pay.

The issue of military pay is important for several reasons. First, it is vital to understand that as chronic as the accounting problems were during the Vietnam War, there were some financial successes. Second, during the conflict, military pay became an issue with which field commanders had to deal. Finally, as had been the case in World War II, the overall success in troop payments was largely due to the extraordinary efforts of military financial personnel.

To be fair, it must be acknowledged that the lessons of World War II did not go completely unheeded. For example, several planners recognized the complexities of financial management during wartime, particularly in a limited war environment, and began initial planning in the late 1950s. The plan was submitted for approval on 18 February 1960, but by May 1961, nothing had happened. In an attempt to force the issue, senior DOD financial management leaders pushed again—but with little success.[23] Perhaps the expectation of unlimited funding, as was the case during previous wars, was a contributing factor. Either way, the net result was the same as had been the case in World War II: financial managers were unprepared to meet the challenges of war.

A unique military pay event during Vietnam was the conversion from US dollars to military pay certificates (MPC), used in lieu of US currency to keep dollars out of the black market. Capt Frank Tuck, USAF, assigned as an accounting and finance officer at Cam Rahn Bay Air Base in 1967–68, was responsible for making the MPC conversions. Tuck recounts, "The process was to actually 'lock down' the base and exchange U.S. dollars for MPCs. As new Airmen arrived in-country, we would take their U.S. dollars and exchange them. When Airmen were due to rotate back to the U.S., we would buy the MPCs back with U.S. dollars."[24]

Captain Tuck described the conversion as very tough because Airmen were constantly moving around the country. He also recalled having to strictly account for MPCs under the watchful eye of "resident auditors." The objective was to conduct MPC conversions for as many and for as much as they could and as fast as possible. During MPC conversion, Tuck recalls not sleeping for more than 36 hours. If for any reason someone had "old" MPCs after a 24-hour period, Airmen had to complete a form explaining why. Tuck said, "There were a thousand legitimate reasons and 10,000 illegitimate—we heard them all."[25] For those assigned to the finance unit, this process was as complicated and tedious as it was unfamiliar. As was the case with many wartime financial duties, this was something they never fathomed happening and had to learn on the fly.

Despite the MPC conversion, fraud was still a major concern. Captain Tuck related a story involving the funds manager for the Cam Rahn Bay hospital. As Tuck was about to complete his tour, local auditors discovered a discrepancy during the hospital cash count. Further investigation revealed that the hospital funds manager had in fact pocketed portions of the fund. Unfortunately for Tuck, this revelation came to light on his very last day in-country. Initially, the auditors wanted to "hold" Tuck to complete the investigation, but he was able to demonstrate to the auditors that the hospital funds manager had indeed embezzled the money. Concerned that yet another revelation might occur, Tuck quickly grabbed his flight back to the United States.[26]

Another Air Force officer, Capt Edward "Ed" Gunderson, was a budget officer stationed at Cam Rahn Bay with Captain Tuck. To replenish cash, Gunderson had to fly to Saigon. Despite the use of MPCs, they still maintained US currency to convert MPCs back to US dollars for rest and recuperation (R&R) breaks, for personnel returning to the United States, and for other such reasons. The Vietnamese banking facility was affectionately referred to as Fort Knox East. Captain Gunderson said, "We would go in the place, get a grocery cart and it was like shopping for money. We would put the money in a parachute bag and go to Tan Son Nhut AB, sit along the flightline and wait for a flight back to Cam Rahn Bay AB. We didn't even go through the passenger terminal or security. We just talked to the pilots and once they recognized our cargo we were let right onboard the airplane."[27]

Captain Gunderson also remembered "C" day when the MPC conversion took place. Although a first for Gunderson, this MPC conversion was the second for Captain Tuck. Over time, the original MPCs made their way into the local black market. As a result, at an appointed hour, a new series of MPCs was issued. The announcement of the new series was transmitted via a classified message. Gunderson found it ironic that although the announcement was classified, local Vietnamese maids were aware of the transition at least a week prior. From his perspective, the war literally stopped on each C day while the exchanges took place. However, he related that by noon of that day, the new series was already showing up in Saigon.[28]

Captain Gunderson related that MPCs were used for everything, including purchases at the base exchange and the clubs. In fact, he recalled that breakfast was 26¢; lunch was 60¢; and supper was 45¢. He also had to secure Vietnamese dollars to pay local employees that worked on base. A frustration for Gunderson was the fact that his wing commander was not very interested in financial management. While the commander was rightfully focused on operations, even when the financial team could get on the commander's schedule to brief the status of funds, he showed little interest. As if things could not be worse for two young captains, Gunderson and Tuck worked for a comptroller that Gunderson described as "something else." His lieutenant colonel boss would put on Airman stripes so he could travel to the Army South Beach and insisted their pickup truck be always available so he could get to a card game and drink.[29] When I asked now-colonel Gunderson, retired, if he felt that the training he received prior to his deployment prepared him for duty in Vietnam, his answer was an emphatic "absolutely not."[30]

Getting the Message: Actions Taken

Something had to give. At the time, the US military essentially prosecuted a war within a war: one against the North Vietnamese and the other against poor financial procedures. In January 1970 a new financial management committee was created. The committee's recommendations resulted in a reorganization that placed critical emphasis and attention on budget management. Yet another group was convened to focus on improving the management of operation and maintenance funds. This effort emphasized improving cost-estimating techniques in support of the appropriations-development process.[31]

A centralized accounting center was established in Okinawa, Japan, to improve accounting procedures and to compensate for the problem of limited financial personnel in country. This development was a good step forward but resulted in two steps backward. The US system of government dictates that once an appropriation is signed into law, it flows from Congress through the DOD to the services and finally winds its way down to the unit that spends the money. That process allows funds to be obligated (spent), recorded, consolidated, and transmitted back up the chain for accountability and control purposes. The following are advantages of this system: expenditures can be tracked down to the individual making a purchase, and financial transactions can be sorted in various ways to provide real-time expenditure data or, in a word, accountability.

Unfortunately, the DOD abandoned that process in Vietnam. Instead, since there was no wartime accounting system to record expenditures, the central finance office in Okinawa sent "suballotments" of budget authority to field commanders for limited purchases. As rudimentary as it sounds, commanders actually had to record purchases on the back of the funding document to maintain the balance in the account. Then, each month the documents were sent to Okinawa to be recorded in the central accounting system. As one can imagine, with $50 million suballotted to the field, a ton of documents flowed between Vietnam and the central accounting function each month.[32]

Another problem was the military stock fund that was used to track the costs of supplies and minor equipment. This fund is a revolving account or working capital fund that pays for the supplies up front and is subsequently reimbursed by the purchasing agency. Unfortunately, poor inventory and cost controls wreaked havoc on this process. The lack of discipline in ordering supplies made forecasting inventory virtually impossible. Consequently, sales data were captured neither promptly nor accurately, resulting in cash shortages and, at times, an illiquid stock fund.[33]

At this point, things had reached a boiling point. The financial situation was in shambles, and immediate change was needed. In 1966 the Army took on the financial problems in the Pacific, conducting an in-depth study. The so-called Brooks study was conducted under the direction of a steering committee composed of Dr. Robert A. Brooks, assistant secretary of the Army for installations and logistics; Gen Creighton W. Abrams, vice-chief of staff; Lt Gen Lawrence J. Lincoln, deputy chief of staff for logistics; and Lt Gen Ferdinand J.

Chesarek, comptroller of the Army. The committee recommended that all financial management systems in Vietnam be centralized and moved from Okinawa to Hawaii. The new Centralized Financial Management Agency (CFMA) established updated procedures and features that improved the financial management and supply requisition process.[34] However, the diversities of supply requirements during a wartime environment strained the system and continued to cause errors in accounting.

Lessons Learned

Ironically, many of the financial lessons from Vietnam paralleled those of World War II, while others were unique. First, Congress exerted itself in a big way as a primary player in funds management during war. In the past, Congress essentially functioned like a rubber stamp for defense requests. However, Vietnam taught the DOD that financial management during war is a two-way street. Explicitly, Congress will provide financial support only if the DOD can demonstrate the prudent use of those dollars.

Second, the social and political complexities and controversies surrounding Vietnam resulted in very fragile public support. As such, the need for policies and systems that accurately manage funds in a battlefield environment was crucial. With public support teetering on the edge, any perception of financial waste or impropriety—whether real or perceived—could have easily pushed that fragile support over the edge.

Third, accounting for expenditures in a war zone is at least as critical as accounting for funds during peacetime. Only accounting and tracking expenditures can provide Congress and the public with a reasonable assurance of financial stewardship. This approach enables the DOD to deliver accurate and auditable war costs that in turn allow Congress to quickly verify and approve budget requests. Also, sound internal controls offer a strong hedge against financial abuse, protect against fraud, and ensure financial integrity. The millions lost through the mismanagement of reimbursements are an example of what can happen when fiscal accountability is not strictly enforced.

Fourth, once again, prewar planning was inadequate. Efforts were made at senior DOD levels to develop financial contingency plans, but such efforts were largely ignored. Moreover, there is little evidence that any efforts were devoted to preparing those financial managers who would actually perform in the war zone. This problem is underscored when one considers that the trend of war fighting is to limit the number of administrative personnel in-theater. Therefore, the task of planning and readiness becomes even more critical to compensate for reduced personnel ceilings. Generally, the problem of preparedness and training boiled down to the same issue as it had during World War II—focusing on peacetime rather than wartime operations.

Finally, the evolution of war-fighting policies and tactics in Vietnam placed a premium on the importance of military pay. The World War II–era "foxhole" environment somewhat lessened the impact of troop payments on the battlefield. However, Vietnam ushered in an age of convenience to the military members that made payday one of their most anticipated events. This change is significant because it placed yet another burden on field commanders to ensure accurate and timely payments.

If the evolution of warfare were to continue on its path, the next war would be limited—perhaps with tentative public support. Further, Congress would demand even more in terms of accountability and prudence. Therefore, at the conclusion of Vietnam, it would appear that the DOD could not afford to continue the mistakes of the past, lest it risk seriously impeding congressional and public trust.

Vietnam revalidated the idea that the impact of poor financial management procedures during war is much more than merely administrative; they exacted a significant price from the DOD. After the war, defense spending declined as a total share of gross national product, dropping from 9 percent in fiscal year 1968—the peak-spending year in Vietnam—to 5 percent in fiscal years 1978 and 1979.[35] While much of this decline was certainly due to the postwar drawdown, "the failure to be 'penny wise' in Vietnam cost the services dearly."[36] Perhaps more importantly, the inability of the DOD to provide prudent financial management during the war reversed a once congenial congressional relationship to an adversarial one.

In this review of financial management during Vietnam, we progressed past the point of historical interest to some alarming trends. The fact that major financial deficiencies still persisted after 20 years of lost opportunities for improvement points out that something was terribly awry. Fortunately, our history of warfare would prove accommodating as the United States would not engage in another major conflict for another 20 years.

As fate would have it, many years later, lieutenant and later captain Larry Spencer would work for Colonels Tuck and Gunderson. These gentlemen were outstanding leaders and mentors for me and many others. Perhaps it was also fate that I would have the opportunity to apply the lessons learned from their Vietnam experiences as a financial manager in war. Roughly two decades after Vietnam, the United States entered war again. This time, it was Operation Desert Shield/Storm. This time I was one of those financial managers thrust into war. As was the case during World War II and Vietnam, US forces were not fully financially prepared to support the war.

Notes

1. SecDef for Service Secretaries and JCS, memorandum,1 March 1965 (quotation), folder Official Correspondence: Army Chief of Staff, Close Hold, box 76, H. K. Johnson Papers, Military History Institute; Leonard B. Taylor, *Financial Management of the Vietnam Conflict: 1962–1972* (Washington, DC: GPO, 1974), 17–18; and Bottomly, Note to Control Division, Meeting of Joint Chiefs of Staff and SecDef w/Amb. Taylor, 29 March 1965 (quotation), folder Vietnam 091 March 1965, box 44, Wheeler Papers.

2. Edward J. Drea, *McNamara, Clifford, and the Burdens of Vietnam, 1965–1969*, vol. 6, Secretaries of Defense Historical Series (Washington, DC: Historical Office of the Secretary of Defense, 2011), 90.

3. Memorandum to SecDef for Pres., 5 July 1962, *McNamara Public Statement*, 1962, 4:1519; and DOD Instruction 7720.6, *Cost Reduction Program Reporting System*, 20 January 1964.

4. Joint Logistics Review Board, *Logistics Support in the Vietnam Era* (Washington, DC: DOD, 1970), 354–70.

5. Drea, *McNamara, Clifford, and the Burdens*, 510.

6. Rivers to Hardy, letter, 28 July 1965, attached to letter Rivers to McNamara, 28 April 1966, folder 400, 28 April 1966, box 7, ISA General files, Acc. 70A-6649.

7. Ibid.; and Hardy to Rivers, March 1966, folder SubCte for Spec. Inv. Rpt. on Military Shortages, Etc. (Comments on Letter from Hardy to Rivers) box 90, ASD(C) files, OSD Hist. (quotations).

8. Office of the Secretary of Defense (OSD), DSS, *Selected Manpower Statistics*, 15 April 1969, 7, box 1127, Subject Files, OSD Hist.

9. Taylor, *Financial Management*, v.

10. Stephan Daggett, *Costs of Major U.S. Wars* (Washington, DC: Congressional Research Service, 24 July 2008), http://fpc.state.gov/documents/organization/108054 .pdf. US Inflation Calculator uses the latest US government Consumer Price Index data published on 15 December 2015 to adjust for inflation and calculate the cumulative inflation rate through November 2015, Usinflationcalculator.com.

11. Holton E. Blomgren, "Comptrollership in Vietnam," *Army Finance Journal*, March–April 1967, 12.

12. Headquarters United States Military Assistance Command, Vietnam, to all units within MACV, chief of staff action memorandum no. 70-44, MACCO-F, subject: Conservation of MACV Resources, 8 April 1970. The Army Task Group conducted its survey from 25 September to 21 November 1967.

13. Headquarters US Army, Pacific, Message GPCO 26099, subject: Loss of Army Resources in Support of Reimbursable Customers, 1 August 1967.

14. Department of the Army, Message DA 818750, subject: Services and Supplies Provided Others, 9 June 1967.

15. Comptroller of the Army, memorandum for the chief of staff, subject: Improvement of Accounting Operations in Vietnam and Elsewhere in the US Army, Pacific Command (CSM 67-350), 15 December 1967.

16. United States Air Force, "Major General Charles D. Metcalf," 1 February 1991, http://www.af.mil/AboutUs/Biographies/Display/tabid/225/Article/106195/major-general-charles-d-metcalf.aspx.

17. Maj Gen Charles Metcalf, USAF, retired, interview by the author, 4 November 2015.

18. Ibid.

19. Ibid.

20. Jan W. Brassem, "The 'Money' Man in Vietnam," *Air Force Comptroller* 1, no. 1 (October 1967): 11.

21. Ibid., 13.

22. John W. Fippen, "Combat Support and the Comptroller," *Air Force Comptroller* 2, no. 1 (October 1968): 2–3.

23. Taylor, *Financial Management*, 5.

24. Col Frank Tuck, USAF, retired, to the author, e-mail, 2 December 2015.

25. Ibid.

26. Ibid.

27. Col Edward Gunderson, USAF, retired, to the author, e-mail, 2 December 2015.

28. Ibid.

29. Ibid.

30. Col Edward Gunderson, USAF, retired, phone interview by the author, 6 December 2015.

31. Taylor, *Financial Management*, 37.

32. Frederick L. Orr, chief, Budget Division, Office of the Deputy Chief of Staff, comptroller, Headquarters US Army, Pacific, Department of the Army, and Maj Gen Leonard B. Taylor, interview, 3 December 1971.

33. Taylor, *Financial Management*, 44–46.

34. Briefing, Headquarters US Army, Pacific, 14 January 1969, 1–3.

35. Office of Management and Budget, "Historical Table 3.2—Outlays by Function and Subfunction, 1962–2020," https://www.whitehouse.gov/sites/default/files/omb/budget/fy2016/assets/hist03z2.xls; and "Historical Table 10.1—Gross Domestic Product and Deflators Used in the Historical Tables, 1940–2020," https://www.whitehouse.gov/sites/default/files/omb/budget/fy2016/assets/hist10z1.xls.

36. Louis C. Seelig, *Resource Management in Peace and War* (Washington, DC: National Defense University Press, 1990), 9.

Chapter 3

Operation Desert Storm
Up Close and Personal

Comptroller General Charles Bowsher said it may be impossible to obtain hard figures because of faulty military accounting systems. The General Accounting Office cannot determine the cost of Operation Desert Storm because none of the military services has reliable systems for managing inventories, procurements and expenditures.

—Kevin Power
"Financial Systems Can't Track War Costs Accurately"

A Ledger in the Sand

The deployment of over 500,000 US troops to Southwest Asia in response to Iraq's invasion of Kuwait was unprecedented. Operation Desert Shield/Storm involved more US forces and materiel than did the Vietnam War during its peak in 1968.[1] The Air Force flew over 65,000 sorties and accounted for 31 of 35 kills against fixed-wing aircraft. It is estimated that during the air campaign, "coalition forces destroyed over 400 Iraqi aircraft, including 122 that flew to Iran, without a single loss in air-to-air combat."[2]

Equally unprecedented were the financial challenges associated with this high-tech war. From determining the costs of war to transitioning reservists to the active duty pay system, Desert Shield/Storm represented a quantum leap in demands for financial management during war. Moreover, the conflict helped define war fighting in the twenty-first century. As articulated by Cong. Bill Gradison (R-OH) during hearings before the Committee on the Budget, "This war against Iraq presages very much the type of conflict we are more likely to confront in this new security era—major regional contingencies against foes well-armed with advanced conventional and unconventional weaponry."[3]

So how did military financial managers respond to warfare in the 1990s? Once again, individual military financial personnel performed admirably. Nevertheless, once more, they were not fully prepared for financial operations when the war began. As painful as the lessons of past wars had been, no substantive improvements in training had been made. As predicted from the Vietnam experience, Congress demanded accurate accountability and valid cost estimates; however, the military financial establishment was neither prepared nor equipped to respond.

When Operation Desert Shield/Storm began, it was my turn in the barrel. I was comptroller of the 4th Fighter Wing at Seymour Johnson AFB, North Carolina. I remember that experience as though it happened yesterday. I took the command flag in July 1990, and on 2 August 1990, I watched closely as Saddam Hussein's forces invaded Kuwait. Since this command was my first, I had big plans to ensure that my squadron was trained and prepared for war, but there was no time.

We were glued to our televisions as talk of war began to ratchet up. In response to the Iraqi invasion, on 9 August 1990, our wing deployed four six-ship flights of F-15E Strike Eagle fighter aircraft to Thumrait Air Base, Oman. The very next day, maintenance personnel set up engine and avionics intermediate-level maintenance facilities, and our medics established clinical facilities.

On 25 November 1990 our civil engineers began construction of a new base in Saudi Arabia. By mid-December, Seymour Johnson personnel, along with 24 F-15Es and 1,270 tons of equipment, moved from Thumrait to Prince Sultan Air Base, Al-Kharj, Saudi Arabia. On 27 December 1990 more F-15Es deployed from Seymour Johnson to Prince Sultan, and by the end of the year, we had two full squadrons of F-15Es deployed and ready to fight.

The air campaign began on 15 January 1991, and, unfortunately, we lost an aircraft and crew to ground fire. Four days later, an SA-2 Guideline missile shot down one of our F-15Es piloted by the 4th Fighter Wing's operations group commander, Col David Eberly (see fig. 4), and his crew member, Maj Thomas Griffith Jr. Both successfully ejected from the aircraft and evaded the enemy for two days before being taken captive as prisoners of war (POW). Colonel Eberly was the senior-ranking allied POW in the Gulf War.[4] He, along with other allies from five countries, was repatriated on 5 March 1991.

Figure 4. Col David Eberly, USAF, a prisoner of war captured by Iraqi forces during Operation Desert Storm, salutes the crowd waiting to welcome him and other former POWs upon their return to the United States. (Record Group 330: Records of the Office of the Secretary of Defense, 1921–2008, National Archives Catalog, https://research.archives.gov/id/6473433.)

The loss of an aircrew followed by the capture of two 4th Fighter Wing Airmen was devastating. As the operations group commander and senior leader in the 4th Fighter Wing, I personally knew Colonel Eberly, and he was as fine an officer and gentleman one could ever know. However, the loss and capture of one of our own stiffened our resolve for nothing less than total victory. As the war progressed, it was inspiring to witness thousands of Goldsboro, North Carolina, residents show their support of the 4th Fighter Wing.

By war's end, our F-15Es had flown 2,172 sorties, striking 2,124 targets in Iraq and Kuwait. These strikes included all-weather night attacks, 595 against airfields, communications facilities, and ammunition storage areas. Occasionally working with Joint Surveillance Target Attack Radar System aircraft, our fighters conducted 391 "Scud-hunting" sorties using low-altitude navigation and targeting infrared for night in western Iraq. In support of ground forces, we conducted 949 strikes using GBU-12 Paveway II laser-guided bombs during "tank-plinking" operations against armored vehicles in the Kuwait area of operations.

During the deployment phase of the war, my comptroller squadron was in full war mode. I was tasked to deploy several financial "paying agents" on the second "chalk" (aircraft sequence) to depart. It is a bit hard to imagine now, but I literally had to fill briefcases full of cash and checks and send them, along with several noncommissioned officers (NCO), off to war. We subsequently deployed several more personnel from my squadron.

I remember briefing my team members on their deployment responsibilities. I laid out their duties, which would include making on-the-spot payments to local vendors for goods and services, providing fund citations for equipment purchases, responding to inquiries from individual members regarding pay and travel entitlements and allowances, cashing checks, and accomplishing basic accounting requirements to track obligations for maintaining status of funds and reporting back to home station.

Dealing with government funds is very serious, and my team listened intently, especially when discussing fiduciary responsibilities. Disbursing agents were appointed on orders to act on behalf of the home station accounting and finance officer. They were legally and strictly accountable to the home station for cash, checks, and funding documents issued to them. Accounting and finance officers are held pecuniarily, legally, and personally liable for funds entrusted to them. Additionally, the agents are responsible for ensuring that funds are used only for those things for which they were appropriated. I was particularly concerned that undue pressure could cause a young NCO to make an unauthorized purchase.

Take, for example, the case in which a commander wanted to use operation and maintenance (O&M) funds to purchase new uniform blouses for women due the local customs that prohibited women from wearing short sleeves. However, O&M funds are not authorized for the purchase of uniform items; rather, a clothing allowance is given to members to purchase uniform items. In this case, a very young NCO had to explain these rules to a senior commander—clearly something this person was not accustomed to doing.

I was also concerned that with no deployable accounting system, managing accounting "paperwork" would be a nightmare—and it was. documents were prepared in-theater in order to make changes to a pay account and mailed back to Seymour Johnson for input to the central pay account. Thus, the normal time span for information sent via mail was often two to six weeks. Relying on trial and error, we started using datafax machines that increased processing efficiency considerably.

The officer in charge of my initial deployed cadre was a young accounting and finance officer, Capt Robin Jones from Washington, DC. During high school and college, she had worked as a cashier in a local Sears store, so she was familiar with managing cash. Additionally, as a lieutenant stationed at San Vito Air Station, Italy, she ran one of the largest cash operations in the Air Force that included foreign currency exchanges. She also trained enlisted "paying agents" to perform cashier duties at remote locations.[5] Even with her extensive cash-management experience, she described the deployment to Desert Shield/Storm as "like nothing I had ever seen or prepared for."[6]

When Captain Jones arrived in the theater of operations, she recalled her first reaction as "stunned." She was particularly struck with how desolate the environment was. The main visual she recalls was a "huge tent city."[7] There was not even a facility out of which to operate. Eventually, a "finance" tent was constructed with two cashier windows and two desks to process financial documents (see fig. 5).

Figure 5. Cashier windows in the finance tent, Prince Sultan Air Base, Al-Kharj, Saudi Arabia

I routinely spoke with Captain Jones during her deployment. As her commander, I was most concerned with two activities that dominated her day: cashing personal checks and paying local vendors for goods and services. We were proficient in neither of these duties because those tasks are not performed during peacetime operations. In short, the day-to-day financial mission at Seymour Johnson bore very little resemblance to the duties of our deployed personnel. Moreover, those individuals had to provide their own security.

I was also concerned about several deployed duties that we did not anticipate, such as tracking and reporting assistance-in-kind receipts and valuing and reporting gifts received from other governments. Since this circumstance was a first for us, there were no established procedures in place. Another challenge was delivering timely leave and earnings statements (LES) to deployed members. Since many deployed personnel were diverted from their original destinations, many were not at the location designated on their deployment orders. Based on this uncertainty, we were lucky to achieve a 60–70% effectiveness rate. Like many of the deployed challenges, we simply figured them out on the fly.

In particular, Captain Jones described vendor payments as a surreal challenge: "Since we carried so much cash, I had to be heavily guarded while being transported downtown. When I arrived at the designated location, as was the local custom, our business was preceded by a few cups of tea and some unrelated conversation. And, since I was a woman, local businessmen would not accept payments directly from me. So, I had to count out the money to one of my enlisted men, who in turn would count out the actual payment to the vendor."[8]

I was fascinated to hear Captain Jones recollect her first encounter with a local businessman. She said the facility looked like any other storefront operation, but there was a room in the back of the store for business. The vendor's dress was traditional for men in Saudi Arabia, and he had a well-groomed beard. The gentleman was very courteous and spoke very clear English. The conversation involved questions like the following: How are you doing? Where are you from in the United States? And the old reliable, how are you enjoying our weather?

Following the short chitchat that Captain Jones relayed, an obvious break occurred in the discussion that meant it was time to get down to business. The vendor presented a voucher outlining the terms of the agreement and payment amount. She read over the document very carefully as the vendor anxiously awaited his payment.

Oddly enough, there was no discussion about not taking payment from a woman—it was just understood that would be the case.[9]

I specifically asked Captain Jones if she was offended by being forced to wear an *abaya* (as many other female military members have done since, see fig. 6) and to adjust to a culture that did not afford her the same respect she was accustomed to in the United States. Her response was that she was not offended. She expressed that although she did not personally agree with such practices, she did respect that, as Americans, we were guests in Saudi Arabia and as such we should respect its customs. As her supervisor, I expected no less. However, she did insist that since she had fiduciary responsibility for the funds, she would personally count payments to local vendors even though the vendor would insist a male NCO recount the payments to him.[10]

Figure 6. Female military members have adapted to operations in Muslim countries, wearing traditional head scarves to adhere to local custom. (In this photo by SrA Rylan Albright, USAF, members of the Provincial Reconstruction Team–Farah's female engagement team discuss the outcome of an all-woman *shura* [meeting] with Abdul Haidari, Shib Koh District subgovernor, in Farah Province, Afghanistan, 10 July 2010, http://usacac.army.mil/CAC2/MilitaryReview/Archives/English/MilitaryReview_20150430_art001.pdf.)

During one of our routine phone calls, I asked Captain Jones what procedures had been established to replenish cash; I was taken aback by her response. She related that getting more cash involved an hour-long drive to Riyadh, Saudi Arabia. Since women were not allowed to drive, she enjoyed riding "shotgun" in the front passenger seat. Since she was required to wear an *abaya*, no one ever knew that she was "packing" a 9 mm pistol under her garment.[11]

One of the memories Captain Jones would like to forget is frequently being shocked awake from a dead sleep as incoming munitions launched toward the base.[12] As was the standard procedure, the sirens would blast, and the entire base populace quickly and efficiently scrambled to the nearest bunker, donned their chemical protective gear, and prayed that the mostly ineffective shelling would once again miss the intended targets.

One of the enlisted men working for Captain Jones was SSgt Leonard "Skip" Sergent, an exceptional NCO steeped in financial management and a joy to work with (see fig. 7). Sergent remembers initially arriving at Thumrait, Oman, to face 128-degree temperatures. Upon arrival at Thumrait, his team was directed to a large, open warehouse that had a scattering of vehicles—a place they called home for the first few days. Initially, they used a corner of the building and secured the funds in a small safe chained to a large support beam. For added security, they surrounded the safe with their cots and slept there each night.[13]

Figure 7. SSgt Leonard "Skip" Sergent

The finance team alternated shifts to ensure that someone was guarding the safe at all times. A few days later, a larger two-drawer safe arrived, and Sergeant Sergent remembers they had to literally flip it end over end to get it into the room. Despite being in a war zone, the team almost immediately began to make routine financial transactions, primarily consisting of travel advances.[14]

As an example of the austere conditions at Thumrait, Sergent recalls flying on a C-130 transport aircraft to Riyadh, Saudi Arabia, to replenish checks. Upon his arrival, a captain who was the local accounting and finance officer met the team. The captain, who obviously was not familiar with the austerity at Thumrait, gave them a hard time about the condition of their uniforms. Sergent informed the captain that all they had at Thumrait was a mop bucket to wash their uniforms.[15]

Unfortunately, time did not allow Sergent to visit the local laundry service. Nonetheless, he did have time to get a quick meal in the dining facility before his return flight was scheduled to depart. When he arrived at the chow hall, he noticed a line behind a sign that read "Eggs cooked to order." Out of curiosity, he got in the line and was shocked to discover that when it was his turn to order, the cook actually had real eggs and not the powered version used at Thumrait. After stuffing himself, he was transported to the departing aircraft by the captain who had questioned his uniform's appearance, and the captain commented that he hoped he would never get assigned to Thumrait.[16]

In December 1990 the 4th Fighter Wing was ordered to redeploy to Al Kharj Air Base in Saudi Arabia. When Sergeant Sergent landed at Al Kharj, the location was barely habitable. The engineers were just beginning the process to wet and roll clay dirt on top of the sandy soil to form the foundation on which to build working and living areas. In fact, there was only one visible hard structure on the entire installation.[17]

Immediately, the finance team was dispatched to the local town of Al Kharj to purchase paper plates, cutlery, and so forth for meals. They initially teamed with deployed contracting NCOs and were billeted in a local hotel until base construction was complete. The finance and contracting team members became excited when they heard that Al Kharj had a bank on the base since its presence would make replenishing cash much easier—or at least that was the initial impression.[18]

Sergeant Sergent decided to make a reconnaissance visit to the bank to scope out its capabilities. When he arrived, it was nothing like he expected or hoped it would be. He actually arrived early before the bank opened and noticed it was a wooden structure with windows that had no bars or doors and, for the most part, appeared rickety and unsecure.

At the appointed opening hour, the banker arrived in a station wagon with a large suitcase-like container stuffed with cash. He informed the finance team that, since he had no safe or vault in the "bank," he transported the funds to and from work each day. Needless to say, the finance team was disappointed. Although they did manage to exchange some foreign currency that day, they had no subsequent dealings with the bank.[19]

Sergeant Sergent noted that things he had taken for granted back home, such as secure storage, were not available in the deployed environment.[20] As the 4th Fighter Wing comptroller, I had conducted deployment exercises designed to replicate the deployed environment. However, the realities of maintaining a 24/7 finance operation in an austere location with limited equipment, facilities, security, and access to cash proved that our training was not adequate.

Once the finance team members set up shop, their hours of operation were 0700 to 1900, seven days a week. They were happy that the engineers had constructed a four-station pay counter with bars and a slot to pass paper and currency. Akin to an old bank in the Western movies, it was functional nevertheless. When they closed the pay window at 1900, they still had several hours of work to balance accounts and to store the funds and pay documents. Daily transactions included check cashing, currency exchange, pay allotments, and advance payments.

Sergeant Sergent also noted that initially traveling outside the base was actually a blessing in disguise.[21] Since in Thumrait they had lived in the same room in which they worked, any distraction away from the daily routine provided a much-needed break from the more mundane financial transaction duties. However, once settled at Al Kharj, the security police allowed them to store their funds in the local armory, boosting their morale considerably.

Like Captain Jones, Sergeant Sergent observed that his deployed duties were nothing like he had been trained to perform. For example, he described his first visit downtown to pay local vendors as a totally new experience. As previously discussed, Captain Jones was not accepted by the local vendors because she wore an Air Force battledress uniform rather than the customary *abaya*. This arrangement led to one of Sergeant Sergent's more interesting purchases of buying 250 *abayas* for the female members of the wing. Additionally, the entire finance and contracting team had to adjust to the local custom of daily prayers since local vendors would not conduct business during those sacred hours.[22]

While assigned to Al Kharj, Sergeant Sergent recalled a situation regarding the donning of chemical warfare suits (fig. 8) that, although initially terrifying, turned out to be quite humorous. When hostilities began, before bedtime on the first night, deployed personnel were instructed to stay close to their chemical gear just in case it was needed. Sure enough, the first alarm sounded around 0100. Everyone hustled to the bunkers, put on their masks, and ripped open the sealed bags containing the prepackaged chemical protective suits. Sergent was just completing the donning of his chemical gear when he noticed that one of our finance troops, SrA Rick Vestal, was shouting obscenities. Since Vestal had his mask on, it was difficult to ascertain exactly what the problem was. Upon closer inspection, Sergent noticed that Vestal's chemical suit was inside out. Apparently, it had been improperly packed. So Sergent and several others quickly, albeit not gracefully, got Vestal and his chemical suit squared away.[23]

Figure 8. US military personnel don partial chemical gear during Operation Desert Storm. ("Chapter 6: The Offensive Takes Shape," 148–49, US Army Center of Military History, 7 June 2001, http://www.history.army .mil/books/www/www6.htm.)

SSgt Robert Caldwell was another of our very sharp NCOs who deployed shortly after the initial finance contingent. He was a contracting specialist who would team with our deployed finance troops. Contracting officer Capt Tim Serfass joined Caldwell. To supplement the funds previously transported by finance, I issued Captain Serfass an additional $1,750,000 in cash and checks. I was nervous about transporting that large amount of currency, so to put my mind at ease, we placed the checks in a briefcase and the $250,000 in cash in a satchel-like bag entrusted to Serfass.

The flight to the Persian Gulf took two days, but Captain Serfass dutifully never let that satchel out of his sight. Each time the plane landed, an armed guard was provided. While in flight, he literally slept with the satchel as a pillow. Like the others on the finance/contracting team, Serfass described the initial bare base as nothing more than a runway. After a tent city was constructed, one of his first purchases was asphalt to cover the sand between tents. He also recalls manually tracking expenditures because there was no deployable system to do so.[24]

Contingency contracting officers (CCO) were required to execute contracts in accordance with applicable policy and procedures to sustain war-fighting operations. These demands forced an inexperienced acquisition team to mature quickly. This maturation process included learning local cultural norms and providing security while concurrently developing business acumen to provide timely and accurate advice to deployed commanders.

In other words, Sergeant Caldwell had to grow up fast. The pace of operations during the initial deployment was blistering. The finance/contracting team essentially had to stand-up a new base from scratch, a process that began with identifying a bilingual consultant with ties to the local community and a guide to help their inexperienced workforce with local customs and courtesies.

The team made contact with the closest US embassy to begin establishing host-nation support agreements and assistance-in-kind arrangements. The embassy was also helpful with identifying trusted suppliers. The team's first priority was to procure basic life-support items such as food, potable water, shelter, sanitation services, laundry and bathing facilities, and force protection. Sergeant Caldwell's biggest frustration was that his deployment kit lacked the appropriate templates and instructions to execute contracts in a timely manner.

Another frustration arose from the team's good intentions to consolidate purchases to save money and buy in bulk. Despite their best efforts, there were no prewar plans or sufficient information-technology (IT) infrastructure and no means to track consolidated purchases on an installation with multiple units assigned from various stateside bases. Since each unit deployed with its own funding-accountability documents, there was no way to consolidate funding into one account for ordering purposes.

Finally, Sergeant Caldwell was particularly bothered by several lapses in ethical behavior among some of his peers. CCOs have an obligation to abide by laws and regulations in the conduct of their procurement duties. However, Caldwell related that there were several documented cases of CCOs violating their ethical duties and regulations by succumbing to the temptation for quick cash.

Sergeant Caldwell also related several examples of just how dangerous it is for contracting and finance teams to operate with large sums of money "outside the wire" of base security. In one instance, base security was tight, so a request for security escort by the finance/contracting team was denied. As an alternative, the team—including Caldwell and Sergent—was issued handguns to provide their own security. Unfortunately, because there were no holsters for their handguns, the team set out to purchase holsters in town. During the transaction, the team noticed several suspicious gentlemen surveying their activity.

Unaccustomed to dealing with potentially life-threatening situations, the team had two choices: confront the suspicious characters or run. Since they were outnumbered, the team members chose the latter. Like sprinters jumping over hurdles, they took off and ran through crowds and several outdoor markets with the "bad guys" in hot pursuit. Following an exhaustive run, their pursuers broke off their chase, and the team members hustled to their vehicle and returned safely to the base.[25]

In another incident, Staff Sergeant Caldwell's love of the National Football League nearly cost him dearly. An NFL playoff game for the American Football Conference championship between the Oakland Raiders and the Buffalo Bills was to be televised locally. As an Oakland Raiders fan, Caldwell scheduled an off-base shopping trip to Riyadh. After shopping, rather than return to the base, Caldwell decided to remain in Riyadh to watch the game. Unfortunately, enemy activity was very intense that night. While the base was generally outside the range of enemy munitions, that was not the case in Riyadh.

Fortunately, Caldwell survived the night, but he will always remember that his Oakland Raiders lost by a score of 51 to 3, that he wore his gas mask and chemical suit the entire time, and that coalition Patriot missiles launched constantly to intercept incoming Scud missiles.[26]

From the very beginning of the deployment and throughout its duration, I stayed in constant contact with the senior financial officer in the theater, Lt Col Emerson Smith, Ninth Air Force comptroller. He had overall responsibility for Air Force financial operations during the war. In an interview with Smith, he relayed that even in 2015 he still thinks about the unique experience of Operation Desert Shield/Storm.[27]

When asked what kept him up at night during the war, Lieutenant Colonel Smith responded it was the lack of experience of deployed financial personnel. He was also very concerned about funds security and accountability of funds.[28] Specifically, in an after action report, Smith concluded that the DOD had designed military pay and entitlement systems mainly for fixed installations during peacetime operations. Thus, financial managers found it difficult to provide responsive or flexible support for such a large operation in an austere environment plagued by limited communications.[29] His report further lamented that finance personnel also encountered challenges in such areas as managing assistance-in-kind support from Saudi Arabia and other nations, as well as issues like funding contracts. In these areas there were no procedures since this was the first time such programs were used. The inexperience and lack of procedures made the job quite difficult.[30]

Certainly, Lieutenant Colonel Smith had a huge responsibility. By October 1990 there were 21 sites staffed with 127 financial managers from seven major commands. They held $60 million in funding authority, $5 million in cash, and over $45 million in checks. At the peak of operations, monthly comptroller activity exceeded 8,000 partial and casual payments and 47,000 personal checks cashed in-theater.[31] In my view, the fact that 127 financial managers supported approximately 55,000 Air Force members—nearly a 1 to 400 ratio—is a tribute to the grit and determination of the deployed financial managers.

Following the deployment, commanders and senior enlisted acquisition leaders lamented over a familiar theme in managing money during war: wartime acquisition training had not been appropriately exercised during peacetime operations. Additionally, deployed CCOs did not anticipate the unique challenges of a war zone. For example, as contingency preparedness transitioned to hostilities, some contractors simply did not report to work; others were not allowed on the base because of the security posture.

During the aftermath of Desert Shield/Storm, acquisition personnel continued to struggle with contacting actions. In some cases, it took more than five years to settle on payment issues and individual claims against the United States. The lessons from our finance/contracting teams' experiences led to a renewed vigor to correct deficiencies. In fact, a training program called "Top Dollar" was developed to provide robust and realistic training scenarios.

Following the war, I had the opportunity to attend several Top Dollar training events. They were very thorough and realistic, including a competition among major commands to add a sense of pride and camaraderie. A typical Top Dollar was held in a "tent city" environment that pitted finance/contracting teams against each other to solve various deployment scenarios. Despite the huge success of the Top Dollar program, after several years it was terminated due to budget cuts.

In addition to deploying my own squadron members, I had to concurrently "out-process" hundreds of Airmen from across the wing, a task that proved much more difficult than I could have imagined. The large majority of those Airmen had not discussed contingency personal financial management with their families; consequently, they did not have checkbooks. Also, based on lessons learned in the past, the Air Force no longer made advance or partial payments. Thus, many of our departing Airmen literally had no money.

Our wing had practiced deployments dozens of times, but we had never actually checked our Airmen to determine their financial viability. However, this was for real—it was showtime—so we had little choice other than at least offer limited advance payments to members on the deployment line. Since we could not force members to take an advance on their pay, though, many arrived in the theater of operations with very little—if any—access to cash.

Alone, this situation may not sound like a big deal. However, when our Airmen arrived initially at Thumrait, Oman, many did not have money for basic necessities such as toiletries or stationery. Since we were in a pinch, several of the deployed senior officers took up a collection and provided temporary loans to those in need. To make matters worse, as our deployed Airmen wrote letters back home requesting blank checks, many neglected to negotiate a "check writing" plan.

In other words, checks written at the deployed location took weeks, if not months to clear the bank back home.

Similarly, as spouses and family members stateside wrote checks, deployed Airmen were unaware of the available balance. As a result, unintentional "bad check" writing became a problem that was exacerbated when the 4th Fighter Wing relocated to Saudi Arabia. Today, checks are no longer a primary means of monetary exchange; however, in 1990, as the wing comptroller, I actually had to conduct training sessions in the base theater on checkbook management.

Once our checks and cash arrived in-theater, I turned my attention to funding the war effort. Although we would eventually be reimbursed for our incremental war costs, accounting for those expenses was another matter indeed. Since there was no deployable accounting capability and keeping in mind we had typewriters on every desk rather than a computer, we were literally forced to keep track of expenditures with makeshift spreadsheets. So as hundreds of thousands of dollars were being spent, those expenditures were captured on hundreds of pay vouchers that had to be mailed back to the home station for processing. That procedure resulted in stacks and boxes full of pay vouchers that we had to input into the home-station accounting system. Compounding the problem was the fact that these boxes were mailed, making an accurate and timely count of war costs nearly impossible.

Mounting Congressional Pressure

The great success of the United States in securing allied funding support for the war has been well documented. Allies contributed over $54 billion toward a total bill of $61 billion. However, not nearly as well documented were chronic problems associated with accounting for and projecting costs for the war. In fact, the inability of the DOD to respond to congressional demands for war-cost data briefly rekindled the old Vietnam-era animosities between Congress and the executive branch. At one point, under intense congressional pressure, the US comptroller general admitted that the Pentagon could not provide accurate war-cost data because of "weak" accounting methods.[32] In desperation, the executive branch adopted a policy of nondisclosure.

The reason for the nondisclosure policy was simple—the DOD had no other choice. Despite the lessons of Vietnam, little improvement had been made to modernize wartime accounting procedures and systems. When asked by Congress to look into the problems of DOD accounting, Charles A. Bowsher, comptroller general of the GAO, responded, "We do not have anything close to exact figures on war costs. I don't think the Defense Department will come up with accurate numbers because of their weak accounting systems. They will do what they normally do—put it on a memorandum and give an approximation. If you expect a detailed accounting of great accuracy, you won't get it."[33] In response, Sen. John Glenn (D-OH), chair of the Governmental Affairs Committee, stated in disgust, "We need it [accurate spending figures] for making decisions. It's prudent to keep track of the bills so we don't get trapped like we did after Vietnam. Last year we asked you [the GAO] to look at DOD's accounting system, and the Air Force system, to put it mildly, was a mess. Can't we get good figures?"[34]

Needless to say, the inability of the DOD to report war costs accurately and the subsequent nondisclosure policy caused a furor in Congress. Cong. Leon Panetta (D-CA), chairman of the House Budget Committee, responded by calling the nondisclosure policy "a very big mistake at a very crucial time. . . . Only when the people understand what they are being asked to do will they unify in the long run behind our efforts in the Persian Gulf. The American people cannot decide to pay the price unless they know what the price is, in lives and dollars."[35] In the end, Congress exerted its power by enacting legislation that forced the DOD to provide monthly reports on war costs.

A direct result of inaccurate war-cost projections was the inability to develop a plan for equity of allied contributions. In other words, once US allies were on board to help defray the costs of the war, a determination should have been made concerning which countries should pay what portion of the bill. The Saudis, for example, were receiving about $70 billion in oil revenues as a direct result of US intervention in the war. Based on those facts, perhaps the Saudis should have been billed based on that direct benefit. Similarly, Japan received nearly 70 percent of its oil from the Persian Gulf.[36]

During a 4 January 1991 House Budget Committee hearing, Cong. Jerry Huckaby (D-LA) stated, "What would be a fair share for the Saudis to pay, for Kuwait to pay, for the Japanese to pay, for the Germans to pay? Shouldn't we have a policy rather than just sending the Vice President around, hopping from here and there and saying, 'Would you please give us some more money?' Shouldn't we be able to elucidate and specify, this in our opinion is your fair share?"[37] The sad truth is that it was virtually impossible to develop a fair-share policy because the DOD could not accurately determine the costs.

In defense of the DOD, poor accounting methods aside, Desert Storm clearly highlighted that modern-day warfare is very expensive and that projecting costs for such conflicts is difficult. Early estimates of the first day of the air campaign ranged from $500 million to $1 billion. During the first 24 hours of the war, thousands of 2,000-ton hard-target bombs were dropped at a cost of $11,000 each. Also, about 100 sophisticated Tomahawk cruise missiles were launched at $1 million each. Fortunately, a substantial Desert Storm cost—jet fuel—was borne by Saudi Arabia. However, considering the fact that the full cost of operating a single F-15 fighter can be as high as $1,200 per hour, the expenses were staggering.[38]

More Problems in Accounting

Figuring out the funding for multiservice, common-use support functions and facilities such as *Stars and Stripes* distribution, certain medical supplies, port handling, and so forth were equally deficient. The lack of a centralized funding source for common-user, in-theater support required each service to identify a funding source and attempt to swap funding documents between services.[39] Since there had been no prewar plan or training to facilitate common-user or common-support activities, wasted equipment and money were the result.

For the Air Force, tracking assistance-in-kind support and gifts from foreign governments exposed a particularly troublesome problem.[40] During the war, financial agents were tasked to value and track assistance-in-kind provided by foreign governments. Donations such as the lease of buildings, facilities, food, and fuel were crucial to the war effort and politically sensitive to Congress. However, this tracking was a tall order for financial agents, many of whom were not familiar with assistance-in-kind procedures. With no prior training or guidance, most were unprepared for the task.

More Problems with Pay

Pay and allowances for reservists during the war were—to put it mildly—a challenge. In fact, most reserve Soldiers called to active duty in support of Operation Desert Shield/Storm experienced some pay-related problems. Also, due to such oversights as excessive pay advances at the mobilization station, liberal casual pay policies, and the lack of a finance data system to track and record such payments on the battlefield (all reminiscent of the situation during World War II), a Defense Finance and Accounting Service (DFAS) study estimated that 35 percent of all reservists released from active duty after the war were indebted to the government.[41]

A GAO audit conducted after the war focused on the fact that activated reservists at each of the five installations visited by the auditors complained of not receiving timely pay and travel reimbursements. A major contributing factor was that many active duty installation finance offices were neither staffed nor trained to handle the increased workload of the new reservists. Also, the audit noted that the reserve units' support personnel, who would normally provide such administrative services for the unit, were not activated.[42]

In another twist, for some reservists the errors in military compensation paled in comparison to the personal financial losses experienced from abandoned businesses back home. Dr. John Roane, a reserve lieutenant colonel and gum-disease specialist from Houston, Texas, remembers a colleague calling Operation Desert Storm "Desert Screw." The colleague's eight-month stint in the desert cost him his $250,000-a-year periodontal practice, $20,000 in legal bills, and his good credit rating. Those practitioners, many of whom had no more than three days to report for duty, were forced to scale back services, close their businesses entirely, terminate employees, and/or pay steeper unemployment insurance.

Of the 30 doctors based at Wilford Hall Air Force Medical Center at Lackland AFB, Texas, who resigned from the Air Force Reserve after the war, 27 stated they left to avoid the risk of another financial loss. Also, in the Air Force the number of Reserve doctors dropped from 349 in September 1990 to 221 two years later. Similarly, the number of Air Force Reserve dentists dropped from 119 to 102 during the same period.[43]

The point is that the president called up over 200,000 reservists for active duty to support the war. However, the military was unprepared financially to accept them. With no comprehensive plan to convert reservists to the active pay system, most found themselves in either one of two undesirable situations: over- or underpaid. Thus, many were in substantial debt to the government following the war. Furthermore, the personal financial loss to professional reservists, such as physicians and pilots, indicated that little financial planning was provided to reservists prior to the war.

Pay for those already on active duty was also not immune from problems. By December 1991, the total debt owed to the government due to overpayments of active duty members reached nearly $80 million. Some members of Congress lamented "that so many individuals could be overpaid by such a large aggregate amount."[44] In a personal message from Gen Norman Schwarzkopf, US Army, commander, US Central Command (USCENTCOM), to Gen Carl E. Vuono, the Army chief of staff during the war, he complained of problems with military pay support and indicated that Soldiers in the field were "suffering" because of it. General Schwarzkopf requested that General Vuono "weigh in" on the problem and reiterated that "our soldiers deserve 100% accurate pay each month."[45]

Congressional conferees blamed the problems with pay on the "turmoil" associated with contingencies like Desert Shield/Storm. Additionally, Congress pointed the finger in an all-too-familiar direction: "The conferees note that Department of Defense finance officials, and not service members, appear to be responsible for the majority of the overpayments."[46] In fact, during Desert Storm, 11,775 Airmen were overpaid an amount of $7.4 million. All told, the DOD overpaid 198,078 service members nearly $80 million.[47]

A lack of understanding of pay and entitlements was a significant contributing factor to the problem with troop pay on the part of Air Force members. For example, basic allowance for subsistence (BAS) is paid to enlisted members who live with their families or those who are single but are authorized the allowance-in-kind for not using the government dining facility. Members with families invariably look at this allowance as part of their normal compensation. When they were sent to Desert Shield/Storm and provided government meals at no cost, their entitlement to BAS was terminated, resulting in a reduction in take-home pay. Many of them did not understand this denial, and some found that their families could not make ends meet without this anticipated money.[48]

Lack of Planning for Victory

At this point, the absence of training and preparedness for war in the financial community should be obvious. Not as obvious, but equally as critical, was the lack of preparedness for victory. When hostilities were officially declared over, the chaos of redeployment was rivaled only by the initial deployment. As troops began to return to home stations in droves, most of them understandably had one thing in mind: going home on leave to be with family and friends (fig. 9). However, if a member failed to "process" through the local finance unit (and many failed to do so), the myriad of combat-related pay entitlements continued to accrue. Therefore, upon return to the home unit from an extended leave period, a number of personnel faced the unpleasant reality of having those payments deducted from their paychecks.

Figure 9. SSgt Robert Caldwell returning from Operation Desert Storm to Seymour Johnson Air Force Base

To head off this problem for the 4th Fighter Wing, I requested, and was granted, permission to board each returning airplane just prior to passenger departure. Since waiting families were anxious to see their returning loved ones, I had less than five minutes to make my case. Regardless of the day or time of passenger arrival, I set up finance tables and implored returning members to take five minutes to ensure that their leave and pay were correct before departing for extended leaves.

Fortunately, the majority of our returning troops accepted our offer of assistance. I vividly remember hundreds of returning 4th

Fighter Wing members hugging their families and heading straight for the finance tables. This practice worked well for our unit, but it was developed on the fly. Nothing in our training suggested that we offer this assistance. Consequently, because many other bases did not adopt this practice, hundreds of troops were indebted to the government following leave.

Determining the cost of redeployment was as difficult as tracking deployment costs. For example, damaged equipment returned from the war needing repair or replacement was chargeable as a Desert Storm expense. However, there were few mechanisms in place to record those expenses. Also, equipment left behind in Saudi Arabia could be replaced with Desert Storm funding. But again, there was no accurate method of tracking and validating those replacement costs. From a budget perspective, it was difficult to separate Desert Storm costs from normal operational costs.

Working the Issues: Actions Taken

In response to concerns raised by USCENTCOM during the war, the director of DFAS established a pay support evaluation team (PAYSET) to review the support provided to USCENTCOM, identify systemic problems, and make recommendations on how to resolve the issues. Of particular concern to the team were reported delays in refunding federal and state taxes withheld, the lack of proactiveness and responsiveness by the stateside finance community in providing policy guidance and procedures, the lack of an in-country pay-change input capability, and the timeliness of implementing war-pay entitlements.[49]

While the PAYSET addressed several financial issues in detail, two were particularly critical to improvements in the future. First, the military pay system that supported thousands of deployed troops during the war was a nondeployable computer system. Therefore, pay changes and updates were made the old-fashioned way—mailed back to home stations where automation support was available. This practice was a particular problem when troops received casual or partial payments in the theater that did not update until several months later. In some cases, the collection action for those payments was delayed until after the individual had separated from service, making actual collection action difficult to complete.[50]

Second, the war clearly demonstrated the need for orchestrated planning across the finance spectrum, including both deployable and sustaining base organizations.[51] Although contingency plans existed, no comprehensive financial war plan bridged the services with DFAS, the operators, and the IT community. In other words, the hundreds of financial personnel that deployed to the Persian Gulf came with no comprehensive plan. Little coordination existed across the financial community to ensure continuity of policies, nor was there a plan for joint financial operations.

The Air Force conducted a similar review after the war and found many of the same problems. First, the Air Force flatly admitted there was an overall lack of prewar preparation and training. When the war began, the Air Force generally deployed paying agents that were experienced primarily in military pay and travel functions. Therefore, these agents were oftentimes unprepared to deal with senior commanders on sensitive fiscal policies. Some also lacked experience with vendor payments, working with contracting officers, accounting for funds, and oversight of morale, welfare, and recreation. Moreover, the deployment scheme was disjointed, causing some locations to be short of financial personnel while other locations had too many.

Second, guidance (or the lack thereof) from higher headquarters was problematic. Direction regarding fiscal issues often came from multiple sources, including US Central Command Air Forces, major commands, DFAS, and home-station commands. Additionally, such guidance was oftentimes late, incomplete, and/or inconsistent, creating conflicts and confusion.[52] Thus, in the absence of a reliable single source of information, paying agents were frequently left to their own devices in determining the legalities of financial transactions and establishing financial operational procedures.

Prior to Operation Desert Shield/Storm, I had not read the financial histories of previous wars. Following my tour at Seymour Johnson AFB, I attended the Industrial College of the Armed Forces (ICAF), where I had the opportunity to do just that. As I read the financial histories of previous wars, I was taken aback by the similarities of the historical challenges to those I had just faced. I wondered why my training had not included those lessons learned. I was disappointed that we literally had to rediscover solutions to financial wartime issues that had occurred in the past. Above all, I wondered if the next generation would make the same mistakes during the next war.

Notes

1. Spencer Tucker, *Encyclopedia of the Vietnam War: A Political, Social, and Military History* (Santa Barbara, CA: ABC-CLIO, 1998), 425. Tucker puts forth the figure of 525,000 in Vietnam in 1968.

2. Task Force Enduring Look, United States Air Force, *Air Force Performance in Desert Storm* (Washington, DC: DOD, April 1991), 2, http://www.dtic.mil/dtic/tr /fulltext/u2/a235941.pdf.

3. House, *Hearing before the Committee on the Budget*, 102nd Cong., 1st sess., 27 February 1991, 6.

4. Michael Wines, "After the War: P.O.W.'S; Ex-P.O.W.'S Offer Accounts of Terror and Torture in Iraq," *New York Times*, 15 March 1991, http://www.nytimes.com/1991 /03/15/world/after-the-war-pow-s-ex-pow-s-offer-accounts-of-terror-and-torture-in -iraq.html.

5. Robin Jones, to the author, e-mail, 16 October 2015.

6. Robin Jones, telephone interview by the author, 16 October 2015.

7. Ibid.

8. Jones, e-mail.

9. Robin Jones, telephone interview by the author, 21 October 2015.

10. Jones, telephone interview, 16 October 2015.

11. Ibid.

12. Ibid.

13. Leonard "Skip" Sergent, to the author, e-mail, 10 June 2015.

14. Ibid.

15. Ibid.

16. Ibid.

17. Jones, telephone interview, 16 October 2015.

18. Ibid.

19. Sergent, e-mail.

20. Ibid.

21. Ibid.

22. Ibid.

23. Ibid.

24. Timothy Serfass, telephone interview by the author, 29 October 2015.

25. Robert Caldwell, to the author, e-mail, 18 October 2015.

26. Ibid.

27. Emerson Smith, interview by the author, 10 November 2015.

28. Ibid.

29. Ibid.

30. Ibid.

31. Office of the Secretary of the Air Force (Financial Management), "Financial Management and Comptroller Desert Shield/Storm Lessons Learned Action Items," memorandum, 13 August 1991.

32. William Hershey, "War's Cost Cannot Be Calculated," *Philadelphia Inquirer*, 24 January 1991, 11, http://articles.philly.com/1991-01-24/news/25819990_1_war-endswar -cost-korean-war.

33. Kevin Power, "Financial Systems Can't Track War Costs Accurately," *Government Computer News*, 4 February 1991, 8.

34. Ibid.

35. Quoted in Fred Kaplan, "White House Refuses to Disclose Desert Shield Costs to Congress," *Boston Globe*, 7 January 1991, 9.

36. Jim Sasser, "Is Uncle Sam Getting Stiffed?," *New York Times*, 19 December 1990, 25.

37. House, *Hearing before the Committee on the Budget*, 102nd Cong., 1st sess., 27 February 1991, 4 January 1991, 20.

38. Karen Riley, "1st Day of Desert Storm Cost at Least $500 Million," *Washington Times*, 18 January 1991, 7.

39. Joint Universal Lessons Learned (JULLS) report no. 62163-79755, *Centralized Funding of Contingency Operations*, 26 June 1991. The author personally dealt with this issue as comptroller for Air Combat Command—specifically for deployed Air Force members at Diego Garcia.

40. Office of the Assistant Secretary of the Air Force (Financial Management), "Financial Management and Comptroller Desert Shield/Storm Lessons Learned Action Items," memorandum, 13 August 1991.

41. "Most Desert Storm Reservists Experienced Pay Problems," *Army Reserve Magazine*, iss. 4 (1991): 7.

42. General Accounting Office, *Operation Desert Shield: Problems Encountered by Activated Reservists*, Report GAO/NSIAD-91-290 (Washington, DC: GAO, September 1991), 7.

43. Soraya S. Nelson, "We Were Just Forgotten: Doctors Say Desert Storm Wrecked Them Financially," *Air Force Times*, 18 October 1993, 22.

44. House, National Defense Authorization Act for Fiscal Years 1992 and 1993, Conference Report to Accompany H.R. 2100, report 102-311, 557–58.

45. USCINCCENT to HQ DA, message 092000Z, April 1991, subject: Army Pay in-Theater.

46. House, National Defense Authorization Act, 558.

47. Defense Finance and Accounting Service, "Desert Shield–Desert Storm Servicemembers' Indebtedness," 19 December 1991, 8–9.

48. Office of the Assistant Secretary of the Air Force (Financial Management), "Lessons Learned Action Items."

49. Defense Finance and Accounting Service, "Pay Support Evaluation Team (PAYSET) Concept of Operations," interoffice memorandum, 25 April 1991.

50. Pay Support Evaluation Team (PAYSET), US Army, *Military Pay Support to the Army: Operations DESERT SHIELD/STORM, August 1990–June 1991* (Washington, DC: DOD, 1991), http://www.dtic.mil/dtic/tr/fulltext/u2/a251327.pdf. I had personal knowledge of this practice as comptroller for Air Combat Command, responsible for processing manual payments for individual members.

51. Ibid.

52. Office of the Assistant Secretary of the Air Force (Financial Management), "Lessons Learned Action Items."

Chapter 4

Operations Enduring Freedom and Iraqi Freedom

Shock and Awe

Following Operation Desert Shield/Storm, I was reassigned from Seymour Johnson AFB to attend the ICAF in Washington, DC. Weary but better for the experience, my deep involvement in Operation Desert Shield/Storm was as draining as it was exciting. Having entered the Air Force as the Vietnam War was winding down, I had completed nearly 20 years of service, a full career for most members, without even talk of a serious conflict. Thus, I reasoned that Desert Shield/Storm was the contingency operation of my generation and that I could get back to business as usual—training for a war or contingency that surely would not come during the remainder of my career. I reasoned wrongly.

After I graduated from the ICAF, I served three successive tours outside the comptroller career field: assignment to the White House; mission support group commander at Tinker AFB, Oklahoma; and wing commander at Hill AFB, Utah. Thus, when I arrived at Langley AFB to serve as the Air Combat Command (ACC) comptroller, I had been out of the financial management business for six consecutive years. Having participated heavily in the development of lessons learned following Desert Storm, I felt confident that the problems I encountered during that war had been corrected. Once again, I was wrong.

Operations Enduring Freedom (OEF) and Iraqi Freedom (OIF) put me squarely in the midst of yet another major war. On 19 March 2003 at 2215 EST, I was glued to my television as Pres. George W. Bush announced to the world that US and coalition forces had begun military action against Iraq. By 1215 EST the following day, antiaircraft fire could be seen rising in the skies above Baghdad. Within an hour, huge explosions began rocking the Iraqi capital, as the Pentagon announced that "A-Day" was under way. The campaign was intended to instill "shock and awe" among Iraqi leaders, and air strikes were launched at hundreds of targets in Iraq. CNN correspondent Wolf Blitzer reported that in his 30 years of experience, he had never seen anything on the scale of the attack.[1]

At once my stress level began to rise as I harkened back to those war days at Seymour Johnson AFB. At an Air Force wing, I experienced war from the tactical level. Now, I would do so at the strategic level. During Operation Desert Shield/Desert Storm, I literally worked around the clock solving financial issues—OEF/OIF would be no different. Ironically, my wing commander at Seymour Johnson during Operation Desert Shield/Desert Storm, Col Hal Hornburg, was now General Hornburg, my major command commander. This war would be our second together.

During the buildup to the war, I had prepped my staff and (ACC) wing comptrollers on what to expect. I also visited Shaw AFB, South Carolina, home of our Ninth Air Force (AF), which would be front and center in the conflict. More specifically, I visited Lt Col Robert Blair, Ninth AF comptroller, and his assistant Capt Shylon "Shy" Ferry, who, although junior in rank, had been seasoned through numerous previous deployments. I did not realize it at the time, but this young captain would turn out to be one of the true financial heroes of the war.

Lt Col Emerson Smith was the primary deployed financial manager for Operation Desert Shield/Desert Storm, but Colonel Blair filled that role during OEF/OIF. When Blair arrived at Ninth AF, he had a staff of five people. After 9/11, his Ninth AF staff quickly grew to 12—with another 50 deployed to the theater. When he deployed, the primary activity he witnessed by financial managers was cashing personal checks and supporting contracting officers making local purchases of services and equipment. Since many of the deployed locations did not have electronic payment options, he was unnerved by the sheer number of cash transactions each day.

Colonel Blair said that the "one hard truth we quickly learned was that the Air Force and home station training for deployed duties was woefully inadequate."[2] He believed that the root cause of this lack of preparedness was the fact that instructors with little, if any, actual deployment experience provided home-station training. To supplement the training deficit, Blair and his staff travelled throughout the area of responsibility (AOR), providing on-the-spot training, most of which covered cashier and account-balancing duties.[3]

When the United States suffered the brutal 9/11 attack, Captain Ferry was deployed to Exercise Bright Star, held every two years in Egypt. Bright Star is a series of combined and joint training exercises led by US and Egyptian forces. Specifically, it was designed to strengthen ties between the Egyptian military and USCENTCOM and to demonstrate/enhance the ability of the United States to reinforce its allies in the Middle East in the event of war. At the time of her deployment, Captain Ferry had no idea that unfolding world events would test that capability in real time. In the midst of the exercise, Bright Star quickly transitioned to direct support of OEF. As such, Egypt became a staging area for transporting equipment forward to the Middle East.[4]

Figure 10. Exercise Bright Star. Traveling at a speed of 300 knots (from left to right), an Egyptian F-16, a US Marine AV-8B Harrier, an F-18, and a French Mirage 2000 fighter attack jet fly over the Great Pyramids of Giza as part of a coalition fly-by during the exercise. (Photo by Cpl Chad H. Leddy, US Marine Corps, http://osd.dtic.mil/home/images/photos/2005-09/index/Hi-Res/1_hires.jpg.)

The Bright Star exercise was scheduled from August to October, but based on the onset of the war, Captain Ferry remained through the end of December. Since Ninth AF would run the "air war" in Iraq, Ferry was thrust right back into the fight when she returned to Shaw AFB. When she reported back home, the staff was mobilizing to deploy forward. Between December and April, I worked with both Colonel Blair and Captain Ferry to identify 120 financial managers from Air Force bases around the globe to prepare for deployment to 16 various Middle East locations.[5]

When Captain Ferry initially deployed forward, she was assigned at Headquarters US Central Air Forces (USCENTAF) forward in Kuwait. When she hit the ground, the work pace was brutal. What little sleep she could get was in a tent, but most of her nearly 24-hour day was spent working out of a small trailer. Her initial duties included purchasing services and equipment from local vendors. As mobilized forces began to trickle in, she literally moved from location to location, filling in until assigned financial managers arrived. Additionally, Captain Ferry became the "on call" trainer in the AOR and was frequently called upon to conduct staff assistance training for arriving financial managers who were struggling to operate in a war zone. In all, Ferry made the rounds to Kuwait, Qatar, Oman, the United Arab Emirates, and Saudi Arabia.[6]

Figure 11. Capt Shylon "Shy" Ferry, USAF, receives an award from Lt Gen T. Michael Moseley

Captain Ferry lamented that "everything was manual. Most financial transactions, like travel vouchers, pay updates, and allotments, had to be boxed-up and shipped back to Shaw AFB." During assistance visits, she recalls finding "deployed financial managers struggling with cashing checks, foreign currency exchange, and tracking assistance-in-kind from allied nations. The fact that wartime financial management is so much different than peacetime operations was a real problem."[7] This situation reminded me of the famous Yogi Berra quotation "It's like déjà vu all over again."

I was surprised to discover that, as was the case in Operation Desert Shield/Desert Storm, financial managers all around the continental United States (CONUS) still filled briefcases with cash and checks for the long trip forward. Portable safes, self-security, austere conditions, and insufficiently prepared deploying financial managers all mirrored my experience nearly 10 years earlier. Nothing significant had changed. Deployed commanders were issued funding limitations, and financial managers had to track expenditures manually. The problem was that our financial training had not prepared deploying financial managers to carry out these wartime tasks.

Same Old, Same Old

During the war, I frequently visited Shaw AFB. During one of my trips, I visited the 20th Fighter Wing comptroller squadron and was stunned. I was taken to a room filled to the ceiling with boxes full of financial documents that had been mailed back from the theater. Several junior enlisted financial managers told me that the sheer volume of work and the difficulty of the task exasperated them. They were concerned that many of the financial documents had been hastily prepared overseas and were very difficult to read and interpret. To make the point, they showed me a routine purchase request. Despite using my best interpretive imagination, I could not figure out what had been purchased or how much had been paid.

This predicament caused late payments that resulted in some very unhappy customers. In one case a major airline providing charter service to and from the theater of operations threatened to cease flights unless it received immediate payment. Again, the documents regarding the flights were late arriving to Shaw AFB and were nearly impossible to interpret. To help with the issue of legibility, we dispatched Captain Ferry to the theater to provide immediate training to agents in the field. To help ease the local workload, I directed the temporary assignment of additional financial managers to Shaw AFB, significantly improving operations.

Lt Col Stephen Tye was the comptroller squadron commander at Shaw. As recipient of the mountain of financial documents from the theater, Tye was frustrated that many of the deployed financial managers were skilled in budget, military pay, and travel pay functions back at their home stations but inexperienced with deployed cash-disbursing duties, vendor payments, or foreign currency exchanges: "The crux of the finance support in the AOR was performing as a conduit between the commander and local contractors. This was very difficult for young financial managers who were inexperienced with complicated contracts. With the combination of a lack of experience and a dynamic environment, it's a wonder how our deployed folks didn't have more Anti-Deficiency Act Violations (the act prohibits exceeding funding limits)."[8]

Lieutenant Colonel Tye lamented that, from a training perspective, the guidance and experience that financial managers received from their home-station units just was not sufficient in a wartime environment. I could tell that he was frustrated with the sheer volume of documents his squadron received each week. Missing documents and poorly prepared forms compounded that frustration. His disgust reached the point that he requested and was granted permission to deploy his own squadron members to the AOR to provide hands-on training and lessons learned.[9]

As I drove back from Shaw to Langley AFB, something that bothered me about the mountain of documents suddenly became clear: we had exactly the same problem during my experience during Operation Desert Shield/Desert Storm. As it turned out, the folks at Shaw came up with exactly the same solution. Rather than rely on mail, they started scanning and faxing the documents. This simple change reduced document processing time from months to days. I specifically remembered documenting this problem in my Operation Desert Shield/Desert Storm lessons-learned report, but apparently the lessons had been either lost or disregarded.

As a result, we relived the same mistakes and lost a lot of time. For example, personnel assigned to Camp Snoopy, Qatar, accumulated documents and cashed checks until a UPS box was full enough to mail—a practice that could take weeks. Also, in some cases the packages were misrouted, arrived "compromised," or did not arrive at all. As one can imagine, this process wreaked havoc on individual member's checkbook balancing. The new system (that should have been the initial one) resulted in cashed checks being scanned and processed in less than a week.

During the war, a deployed commander sent an emergency e-mail to the USCENTAF commander concerning the fact that many of his deployed Airmen's pay entitlements had not been started, a problem that would affect their W-2 forms. This error was caused by simple tactical exchange of data between finance and deployed Airmen assigned to Personnel. In a comedy of omissions, deployed personnelists failed to notify the finance office of those arriving in-country, and deployed financial managers simply did not bother to ask. Consequently, several general officers, senior executive service officers, colonels, and others spent countless hours at home stations sorting through and processing the appropriate tax information.[10]

I was one of those colonels working this matter and many other financial issues. Frustrated over the lack of progress since Operation Desert Shield/Desert Storm, I was determined to do something about it. Working with the Ninth AF staff, we created a one-week predeployment course—the Southwest Asia Finance Seminar—at Shaw AFB to train all deploying financial managers. Class size was typically 30–50 students and was conducted two to three times per year. The hastily developed course was taught in base education facilities that were normally used for evening college courses. The course curriculum included deployed cashier duties, account balancing, contracting support, in-kind support, and host-country culture.

Since we had to establish the course in a hurry, the Ninth AF staff was forced to pull double duty as instructors. Occasionally, I also filled in as an instructor. When I cut the ribbon on the inaugural course, I vividly remember my opening comments to the class: "The first thing you all must understand is financial management during war is very different from your garrison experience." The deployed USCENTAF commander, Lt Gen T. Michael Moseley, deemed the course a huge step forward and an "order of magnitude plus-up."[11]

One of the students who attended the deployment course was Capt Louise Shumate. Following the course, she deployed to Ahmed Al Jaber Air Base, Kuwait, in 2001. She recollected, "If it were not for the training received at Shaw AFB prior to my deployment, I would have really struggled."[12] Shumate encountered an unusual situation in that the cashier operations were conducted in the medical facility to take advantage of its secure area for pharmaceuticals. It was tenable to cash checks alongside personnel dispensing medications; however, each day, the financial specialists had to return to the finance facility to "balance out" their accounts.

Accounting for funds spent on major projects was a concern. Captain Shumate had no automated system to track projected expenditures and to ensure that fiscal limits were not exceeded. Based on her training, she established a monthly funds report that, albeit a manual solution, provided the necessary accountability. Despite the predeployment training, she struggled mightily with "missed meals." When Air Force enlisted members are assigned at their home station, they are entitled to a monthly BAS payment. However, if meals are provided during a deployment, including meals, ready to eat (MRE), the BAS entitlement is adjusted accordingly. Not only was this predicament a "morale killer" for the troops but also it was a nightmare for financial managers to track and compute.[13]

Figure 12. Finance customer service. CMSgt Shelina Frey, USAF, 380th Air Expeditionary Wing (AEW) command chief, works the finance customer service desk with SrA Steven Nelson, 380 AEW finance technician, at an undisclosed location in Southwest Asia, 4 March 2013. (Photo by TSgt Christina M. Styer, USAF, http://media.defense.gov/2013 /Mar/17/2000066964/670/394/0/130304-F-ME639-013.JPG.)

When I returned to ACC headquarters from opening the predeployment training course at Shaw AFB, I attacked the financial challenges of the war with a vengeance. To track and fix problems, I established a 24/7 contingency action team with the sole purpose of theater financial support. Recognizing that rapidly changing wartime pay entitlements would complicate pay calculations, we galvanized DFAS support to update pay records quickly. At times, I was overwhelmed at the sheer number of financial problems that hit us. On one occasion, I received a personal phone call from the deployed commander at Diego Garcia. Since his bomber wing shared the small atoll with the Navy, his troops wanted the same entitlements. For example, the Navy provided haircuts and the *Stars and Stripes* newspaper free of charge. Unfortunately, there was no such policy for assigned Airmen.

I was also under the gun to get funding for firepower on the battlefield as quickly as possible. For example, I had to really hustle to get $123 million to pay for getting the U-2 aircraft, the light Predator remotely piloted vehicle, and the heavier remotely piloted Global Hawk into the fight. We also had to find $78 million to integrate Federal Aviation Administration radars into Operation Noble Eagle (ONE) operations. Additionally, integrating Air Reserve Component support into OEF and ONE operations drove an unanticipated bill, so I had to source an additional $395 million.

Seemingly insignificant issues quickly became significant, including the use of government purchase cards (GPC). Because financial managers deployed to the theater with individual GPCs from their home stations, legitimate war charges were billed back to the home-station budget rather than being coded and charged against the operation. To solve this dilemma, one of my pay experts developed a centralized Southwest Asia charge card that isolated and appropriately tracked and charged war expenses. As was the case during previous conflicts, tracking reimbursements and assistance-in-kind charges was very problematic. This dilemma was a big deal for my command because we believed that the Air Force was absorbing more than its fair share of costs. After a personal phone call with my Army counterpart, we agreed to deploy an Air Force financial officer to manage those charges personally.

Another seemingly small issue involving coinage in the theater became front and center on my desk. Deployed military finance offices normally support coinage needs; however, due to costs in shipping and issues with customs security, we could not provide metal coins to remotely deployed locations. Working with the Army and Air Force Exchange Service (AAFES), we came up with a unique solution. To replace the heavy coins, AAFES developed a much lighter version called "pogs," which looked like coins but were made of card stock.[14] They were produced in 5¢, 10¢, and 25¢ denominations. Pogs were produced in Dallas, Texas, and shipped to the Exchange Kuwait Accounting office for distribution to applicable sites. Pogs were treated as cash and were essentially used like gift certificates.

Grading Our Work

Like preceding wars, OEF and OIF consumed a large amount of US treasure. As a result, following major combat operations, Congress tasked the GAO to examine how those funds were managed. The results of the GAO report landed on my desk in spring 2002. As I read the GAO audit, it simultaneously caused quite a stir in the Pentagon. Specifically, the GAO was asked to determine whether the money spent in Southwest Asia was appropriate and whether the DOD provided sufficient oversight to ensure that expenditures were necessary and proper. Since more than 80 percent of the expenditures were attributed to the Army and Air Force, the review was confined to those two services during fiscal years 2000 and 2001.

Most of the Air Force expenditures focused on OEF and OIF and thus belonged to my command, putting us in the spotlight. While the GAO reported that most contingency expenditures were appropriate, it stated that roughly $100 million of the $2.2 billion total spent during that period were spent on "questionable" or unnecessary purchases. My initial take on the matter, considering past financial performances during war, was that—while it was imperfect—getting 95 percent right was not bad. However, that was not the initial reaction from either the Pentagon or Congress.

The GAO placed the questionable purchases into three categories:

1. Expenses that did not appear to be incremental costs—that is, costs that would not have been incurred were it not for the operation. For example, one unit completely rebuilt vehicles that were not used in support of a contingency operation.

2. Repetitive expenditures for items already available in theater. For example, four successive Army units deploying to Bosnia spent a

total of $2.3 million on similar computer and office equipment without attempting to share or reuse the equipment.

3. Seemingly unneeded expenditures, including items such as cappuccino machines, golf memberships, and decorator furniture.[15]

Upon closer examination, it was determined that many of the "seemingly unnecessary" purchases were in fact legal and, in the judgment of deployed commanders, appropriate—particularly considering the fact that most of the purchases involved morale and welfare equipment. However, just as I was breathing a sigh of relief, I realized that the larger and clearly more intriguing issue was the GAO's determination that the DOD had failed to provide the appropriate guidance and oversight as to what *should*, rather than what *could*, be purchased.

There were essentially no consistent standards or levels of effort defined to guide the expenditure of funds during this extended contingency environment. Said another way, the DOD had not clearly delineated how much is enough with regards to investing money into a deployed base. Whereas this revelation took much of the heat away from our command, it did cause the Air Force to examine the issue in much more detail.

A key concern was whether bases in a contingency environment should have the same recreational conveniences as a permanent base, including access to libraries, computers, gyms, movies, and so forth. Regardless of which side of the argument one supports, the point remains that the DOD had not resolved these questions and provided no guidance on funding limits for contingency operations. Rightly or wrongly, individual deployed commanders, along with their financial advisors, made the call. Specifically, the GAO questioned why commanders, with the consent of deployed financial managers, needed to purchase items such as VCRs for each billeting room, cappuccino machines, and sumo wrestling suits.

Other purchases raised even more concerns. For example, deployed Air Force personnel residing in the contingency dormitory at Aviano Air Base, Italy, were provided sightseeing trips to Venice and other locations on weekends. Ordinarily, scheduling morale trips for deployed personnel in a contingency environment is absolutely allowable and proper. However, it was unclear to the GAO why personnel in Aviano, a noncombat zone where people are free to travel about the area while off duty, were provided this service, with the cost charged to the contingency account. During the GAO audit, Air Force officials advised that such tours had been discontinued.

The GAO concluded that limited guidance and oversight, combined with a lack of cost-consciousness, contributed to these questionable uses of contingency funds. Very little visibility existed above the deploying unit level over how contingency funds were used. The DOD, service headquarters, and their major commands received only summarized cost reports from their cost-reporting systems. The military services and their major commands did not receive detailed lists of goods and services actually purchased, nor did they make periodic visits to individual units to examine expenditure records. In addition, the DOD did not have an overview process to evaluate and examine contracts awarded—many of which were very expensive and involved foreign vendors.

The GAO believed that another clear contributor to these questionable purchases was the fact that field commanders had no financial incentive to minimize contingency costs. Since contingency funds generally do not affect base budgets, deployed commanders essentially operated without fiscal constraint. This situation reduced the financial incentive to minimize costs because commanders were not required to weigh funding for contingency operations against competing budgetary priorities.

To be fair, I am not personally convinced that commanders need that type of "pressure" on resources during an active wartime environment—that is not, however, to suggest a return to the days of World War II and the open checkbook. But I do believe that some level of morale and welfare support is necessary and proper; it is just a matter of how much is enough. The real culprit in this case was not the commander but the lack of headquarters' oversight and guidance.

The GAO recommended that the DOD expand financial regulations to include more comprehensive guidance governing the use of contingency funds. At a minimum, the audit advised that the guidance include examples of what contingency funds can and cannot be used for and what units should do with equipment procured with those funds when the equipment is no longer needed. Congress intended to make a point with the GAO audit, to ensure the DOD got the message, as the following language that appears in the *Report of the Committee on Appropriations* for the DOD Appropriations Bill of 2003 clearly indicates:

The Committee is committed to providing the necessary funding for contingency operations that the military forces of the United States are directed to undertake. In order to ensure all required funds are available to the armed forces, the Committee relies on information provided by the administration, both in estimating resources required, and in evaluating the adequacy of provided funding as operations are executed. In May 2002 the General Accounting Office reported, based on an analysis of costs claimed by the selected Army and Air Force units during fiscal years 2000 and 2001, that while most contingency operations expenditures were appropriate, over $100,000,000 were spent on questionable items that were not incremental costs of operations, for equipment that was already available in theater, and for frivolous items including cappuccino machines, golf memberships, and decorator furniture.[16]

The final outcome of the GAO audit was more than a mere mention in the Congressional Record; in fact, the committee penalized the DOD by summarily decrementing the budgets of the Army and Air Force by $50,000 each. For my part, although I am not a micromanager by nature, I was forced to be one. Since the Pentagon was going to hold me responsible for purchases in the theater, I needed a mechanism to track expenditures. So we created a process whereby I reviewed every line item purchased in the theater. Even though this ritual was oftentimes painful, on more than one occasion my eyebrows were raised as I tried to justify why a specific purchase was necessary. In those cases, we quickly followed up and in some cases cancelled the purchases.

During war, flexibility is allowed between appropriated and nonappropriated funds (NAF) for morale, welfare, and recreation (MWR) purchases. Specifically, appropriated funds are authorized for services' activities, including personnel, lodging facilities, food services, libraries, and community activity centers at deployed locations. However, US Central Command Regulation 28-1, *Morale, Welfare and Recreation Programs and Policies*, 28 February 2001, authorized resale operations at the lowest-possible prices with a markup not exceeding 25 percent and required that all earnings from resale operations (profits) be reinvested in the AOR deployment program.

An Air Force audit examined theater MWR expenditures to determine if regulatory guidance had been followed; the results were not flattering.[17] First, US Air Forces Central Command (USAFCENT) officials did not use retained earnings to support AOR services' activities. Rather, services personnel continued to spend appropriated money for MWR activities while they invested most of the earnings back in the CONUS. For example, NAF profits in the AOR were used to fund golf course equipment for Dyess AFB, Texas, and sports bar equipment for Nellis AFB, Nevada. Additionally, AOR NAF profits were used to renovate the Langley AFB officers' club and recreational vehicle sites at Davis–Monthan AFB, Montana.

Second, services personnel neither consistently nor appropriately priced resale goods. For example, at Al Dhafra Air Base, United Arab Emirates, wholesale beer prices were increased by an average of 85 percent while other items such as hard liquor were increased by an average of over 500 percent. When questioned as to why regulatory guidance was not followed, USAFCENT officials admitted they were not aware of the regulations governing AOR profits during wartime.

Yet another earlier, prewar GAO audit confirmed that estimating the costs of war remains a troublesome area for financial managers.[18] For the Air Force, the problems involved both overstating some costs and understating others. On the one hand, the Air Force overstated reported flying-hour costs by $67 million in fiscal years 1994 and 1995. For the most part, this snafu was because the Air Force failed to adjust its reported fiscal year 1994 flying-hour costs by the value of free fuel provided by Saudi Arabia.

On the other hand, the Air Force understated military personnel costs by $81 million of such incremental costs as imminent-danger pay and family-separation allowance. Air Force officials said they were unaware of the requirement to account for these costs even though those costs were reimbursed as a war expense. The report went on to say that neither the DOD nor the services had sufficient guidance or instructions on which costs to include, how to calculate them, or how to apply generally accepted internal controls.[19]

A verbal exchange between Senator Robert Byrd (D-WV) and Secretary of Defense Donald Rumsfeld during a hearing before the Senate Committee on Armed Services in July 2003 offers insight into the uncertainty over war costs:

> Senator Byrd: All right. Mr. Secretary, what is the current monthly spend rate to support our ongoing military operations in Iraq?
>
> Secretary Rumsfeld: It's a combination of appropriated funds as you, sir, know better than any plus the expenditures of funds that are taking place from Iraqi frozen assets, from Iraqi seized assets, and from U.N./Iraqi assets under the Oil for Food program. I can certainly have Dr. Zakheim come up and provide a very precise answer as to what's currently being spent.

Senator Byrd: Do you recall a figure? Can you give us an estimate? I've heard a figure of $1.5 billion a month.

Secretary Rumsfeld: I would not want to venture a guess and be wrong, sir.

Senator Byrd: Somebody ought to know.

Secretary Rumsfeld: . . . I wish I were able to do that, but it falls into a variety of different baskets under our appropriated funds.

Senator Byrd: I understand that, . . . but I've been around here going on 51 years. I'm on the Appropriations Committee and we want to fund our military certainly and meet the needs, but there must be some figure, some amount, that we can cite as an amount that we're spending monthly in Afghanistan and the same with respect to Iraq.

Secretary Rumsfeld: I'm sure there is, and we'll get it for you.[20]

Enough Is Enough

After reviewing these audits, I was determined that enough is enough. This lack of financial preparedness during war had to stop. With the experience of two major wars under my belt, I developed and delivered a problem/solution briefing to Assistant Secretary of the Air Force (Financial Management and Comptroller) Michael Montelongo. Having just "lived the dream" of financial management during war himself, it did not take much to convince him that immediate action needed to be taken, and he backed me 100 percent. As a result, he convened a worldwide financial war planners' conference to identify lessons learned and develop solutions to improve financial management on the battlefield.

Following the conference, Air Force Financial Management leadership vowed to make a change. The summary of the conference results perfectly captured the summation of my overall concerns:

Financial management during wartime is just as important, if not more important, than in peacetime. Support for deployed operations is particularly important because it demonstrates the protection of United States interests and is a comptroller's number one core competency. Yet, in times of war, the comptroller community is consistently unprepared to execute its primary function—support deployed operations. Lessons learned tend to be the same lessons from previous conflicts and operations. Despite numerous attempts to fix the process, warplanning continues to be overlooked and undervalued as a core competency within the comptroller community.[21]

The conference report presented another startling and disappointing finding. Following Operation Desert Shield/Desert Storm, in 1995, a group of financial war planners had also convened a conference. The results of that conference produced many of the same recommendations. Unfortunately, there was no evidence that those recommendations were ever implemented. The conference report noted that what was lacking in the past was a systematic plan coupled with total comptroller community focus on implementing the recommendations. Consequently, a primary action item of this report was to ensure that the recommendations were implemented.

The "get well" plan was very comprehensive and contained many recommendations for improvement. Among these, the very first recommendation was to "determine who is in charge." During the war there were multiple locations staffed with financial managers from multiple commands. Thus, deployed members "reached back" to individual home stations for assistance. As one can imagine, there was no consistency in financial guidance. I specifically briefed the item "need to establish better guidelines for use of the Government Travel Card," based on the confusion over charges that I experienced.

"Need to ensure that financial managers are included in the joint planning process." Again, I briefed this item because oftentimes financial management is an afterthought during war planning. As a result, initial deploying forces arrive in-theater without the supplies and equipment needed to prosecute the war. My specific recommendation was to include financial managers on the initial flow-of-forces plan. "Need to establish new training standards for deployed personnel." Specifically, there was a suggestion to develop a financial contingency course. "Need to establish Air National Guard and Reserve funding guidance." "Improve fundamentals." This recommendation addressed the need for a central financial control location in the CONUS. Again, it was noted that this recommendation was suggested following Operation Desert Shield/Desert Storm.[22] In my judgment, the recommendations were germane; however, they were all too familiar: I had heard them all before.

I was encouraged that the financial management leadership took this process so seriously. In fact, the improvement plan included milestones, responsible individuals, and suspense dates. However, shortly after the conference, others and I moved on to other assignments. I was transferred to Headquarters Air Force Materiel Command at Wright Patterson AFB, Ohio. My new job was completely outside the financial management community, so I quickly lost track of the conference report actions. The drive from Virginia to Ohio took me through the mountains of West Virginia. Driving up and down the steep inclines and declines reminded me of the ups and downs of the war.

It also reminded me that as much work as others and I had put into fixing the financial problems of war, I had seen this movie before. Working through the recommendations for improvements served as a painful reminder to me that I had developed many of the same recommendations before. It seems that, for some unknown reason, we get concerned with money and war only when the fighting begins. Despite the painful lessons of the past, those lessons are placed on a shelf to collect dust. I privately hoped this time would be different, but based on past experience, I was not optimistic.

My country called on me twice to serve during war, and despite the fact that I certainly do not like war, I was privileged to do my duty. There were proud moments as I witnessed US forces completely dominate our adversary. However, those days and nights I spent fighting through the myriad of financial issues were tough. As a financial leader, I always said that our job was to take care of pay for our troops so they could focus on the mission. However, to have our troops worried about W-2 forms and coinage for Base Exchange purchases in the middle of a war illustrated that we had not done our best. However, the brightest times were my personal interactions with deployed financial managers. We sent them off to war without sufficient training, and despite the hurdles, they adapted and overcame.

I have no idea when or where the next generation of Airmen will go to war. However, history is clear on one thing: there will be other wars. If history is destined to repeat itself, Air Force financial managers in the future, who will have little knowledge about the experiences of OEF and OIF, will relive the lessons I learned all too well—possibly twice! The good news is that it does not have to be that way. We can stop this pattern of inadequate training. Will financial managers overcome the challenges of war in the future? Of course they will. However, the experience need not be as painful as the one encountered by their predecessors. As I step out of the Air Force, I will not have to face war again. However, I do want to leave those coming behind me a road map for improvement. Whether or not those following me will change history, only time will tell.

Notes

1. "'Shock and Awe' Campaign Underway in Iraq," *CNN Student News*, 22 March 2003, http://edition.cnn.com/2003/fyi/news/03/22/iraq.war.

2. Robert Blair, to the author, e-mail, 30 November 2015.

3. Ibid.

4. Shylon Ferry, interview by the author, 27 November 2015.

5. Ibid.

6. Ibid.

7. Ibid.

8. Stephen Tye, to the author, e-mail, 11 December 2015.

9. Ibid.

10. Edward E. Marshall Jr., to the author, e-mail, 5 December 2015. Then-captain Marshall was chief of comptroller war plans and contingency operations, Financial Management Directorate, Air Combat Command.

11. Comments by Lt Gen T. Michael Moseley in Officer Performance Report for Capt Shylon Ferry, 7 August 2003.

12. Louise Shumate, to the author, e-mail, 30 November 2015.

13. Ibid.

14. The acronym has an interesting origin. The original POG "coins" were the caps from a common fruit drink of the same name produced by Meadow Gold Dairies and sold at AAFES outlets. The main ingredients in the drink are passion fruit, orange, and guava juices—thus, the acronym POG. Even after AAFES began printing its card-stock version of the currency, the name stuck—albeit in a lowercase form: pogs.

15. General Accounting Office (GAO), *Defense Budget: Need to Strengthen Guidance and Oversight of Contingency Operations Costs*, GAO-02-450 (Washington, DC: GAO, May 2002), 2, http://www.gao.gov/assets/240/234701.pdf.

16. House, *Report of the Committee on Appropriations on Department of Defense Appropriations Bill, 2003*, 107th Cong., 2nd sess., 25 June 2002, 43, https://www.congress.gov/107/crpt/hrpt532/CRPT-107hrpt532.pdf.

17. Air Force Audit Agency Report, *United States Air Forces Central Area of Responsibility Services Financial Activities*, F2010-0001-FD4000 (Washington, DC: USAF, 7 October 2009).

18. General Accounting Office, *Report to Congressional Requesters: Contingency Operations, DOD's Reported Costs Contain Significant Inaccuracies*, GAO/NSIAD-96-115 (Washington, DC: GAO, May 1996), http://www.gao.gov/assets/160/155431.pdf.

19. Ibid.

20. Senate, *Hearing before the Committee on Armed Services: "Lessons Learned" during Operation Enduring Freedom in Afghanistan and Operation Iraqi Freedom, and Ongoing Operations in the United States Central Command Region*, 108th Cong., 1st sess., 9 July 2003, https://www.gpo.gov/fdsys/pkg/CHRG-108shrg96501/html/CHRG-108shrg96501.htm.

21. Gregory L. Morgan, "Comptroller Warplanning Implementation Plan: Detailed Outline" (working draft, Headquarters USAF, 30 March 2002).

22. Ibid.

Chapter 5

What Did We Learn?

A Path Forward

Having traced financial management through World War II, Vietnam, Operation Desert Shield/Storm, and Operations Enduring Freedom and Iraqi Freedom, this article reveals painfully straightforward conclusions and observations. The first conclusion is undeniable: sound fiscal management in a wartime environment is extremely critical. Whether it is paying the troops accurately and on time, properly estimating the costs of war, maintaining appropriate internal controls, paying local vendors accurately, or understanding local customs with regard to financial transactions, it is not only money that make wars go smoothly but also the management of that money.

Second, the fact that financial operations during peacetime are so much different than fiscal management during wartime is a major contributor to the lack of wartime preparedness of military financial managers. During garrison operations, these managers do not cash personal checks. In fact, in such settings, handling and accounting for cash are rare. Similarly, paying local vendors for goods and services and conducting foreign currency exchanges are rare during peacetime operations. Yet, during war, these activities are the norm rather than the exception.

Third, the lack of automation support during deployed operations has plagued financial operations during war throughout history. During peacetime, financial operations—everything from budget preparation to funds distribution, vendor payments, and maintaining accounting records—are all automated. Unfortunately, this is not the case in a deployed environment. The lack of a deployable financial system has stymied financial performance during war, over and over again.

Fourth, higher headquarters guidance and direction were either inadequate or nonexistent. It is hard for me to comprehend that fact, but it is as much the case today as it was during World War II. I witnessed it during Operation Desert Shield/Storm, and I lived it again during OEF/OIF. During each major war examined here, financial managers showed up on the field of battle without the proper guidance and tools to do the job. The General Accounting Office, the

Department of Defense Inspector General, and Air Force audits have continually validated this shortfall, but their recommendations appear to have gone unheeded.

Fifth, the lack of training and preparedness stands out like a sore thumb. Otherwise stellar financial managers are simply not provided the depth of training needed to perform successfully during war. From paying the troops accurately and on time to dealing with vendors from a variety of nations and cultures to understanding unique obligations such as computing and tracking in-kind support, each war told the same story: deployed financial managers were not sufficiently trained.

Sixth, accurately determining the costs of war is critical to securing congressional and national support, but the DOD is simply not equipped to provide such data. The phrase "weak accounting systems" was echoed throughout each war and should come as no surprise for two reasons: (1) Air Force accounting systems are old and outdated and (2) the Air Force eliminated cost-estimating capabilities at the wing level years ago, eliminating that expertise. Even with that reality, history shows that major commands and the Pentagon struggled mightily to develop accurate cost estimates, much to the dismay and anger of Congress.

Finally, wars are generational. Having spent nearly 44 years on active duty, I experienced war twice—but I am the exception. History shows that military financial managers may experience one actual war during their careers. In terms of experiencing wars overall, we are fortunate they do not occur more frequently. In terms of war preparedness, it is no wonder the financial lessons of war are learned over and over again.

The preceding chapters evaluated financial performance during war, making a strong case that deployed military financial managers were not fully prepared to operate either efficiently or effectively in-theater. Prior to World War II, there was no plan for financial operations during war. People were trained and systems were developed with a peacetime focus. Decision makers theorized that those peace-time skills and tools would easily convert to accommodate war. Unfortunately, history proved that theory wrong.

Financial managers entered World War II with little clue about how to execute fiscal management on the battlefield. Not only were they late arriving to the theater but also they were ill equipped and poorly prepared when they got there. Cases of inaccurate payments or no payments at all were common throughout the course of the war. With no doctrinal guidance or fiscal controls, fraud and waste were rampant.

A postwar report on financial conditions concluded that no one had knowledge of expenditures during the war. The services spent $176 billion, but no one knew exactly how, when, or where the funds were consumed. Interestingly enough, although the financial lessons of World War II were chronic and undeniable, only roughly 20 years later during Vietnam, comptroller leadership had still not heeded those lessons.

Vietnam caught the financial community yet again unprepared. During the early stages of the war, it appeared that the "open check-book" policy of World War II would once again be the norm. However, to keep spending under control, the secretary of defense imple mented cost-saving measures that were later overruled by Congress. As the war progressed, costs began to escalate, and public support for the war soured. As a result, Congress reversed itself and demanded accountability for the huge emergency supplemental requests. Having done little to correct the problems of fiscal management in the past, the DOD could not deliver. This inability to manage money during war so incensed the Congress that an undeniable wedge of distrust resulted. What followed was a continuum of animosity over reported cases of excessive waste.

Deployed financial specialists, trained in peacetime operations only, had to learn battlefield operations on the job. The philosophy of conducting military operations using a base-camp strategy placed a premium on individual troop pay, which consumed valuable time from field commanders. Although the nature of the war in Vietnam was quite different from that of World War II, the problems in financial management were almost identical. Prewar planning was virtually nonexistent; financial personnel were not sufficiently trained, and financial systems were not designed for a war zone. Requirements such as converting US dollars to military pay certificates caught financial managers by complete surprise, forcing them to write the rules as events occurred.

The next big test of financial support during war occurred 20 years later during Operation Desert Shield/Storm, and I got the opportunity to witness wartime financial management up close and personal. With nearly two decades to improve upon the disappointments of the past, one would certainly assume that the financial community could respond to this benchmark in modern-day warfare. However, despite the lessons of World War II, poor marks during Vietnam, and advances in fiscal technology, the comptroller community entered Operation Desert Shield/Storm nearly as unprepared as before. Once again, financial priorities had been focused on peacetime operations, not war.

Despite an improved relationship between Congress and the DOD, frustrations over the inability of the military to provide war-cost data for Desert Shield/Storm threatened a return to the old animosities of the past. Blaming shortfalls in accountability on "weak" accounting systems, particularly in the Air Force, the DOD simply had no way to accurately track the costs of the war. Thus, in the end, the DOD provided the only data it could—estimates and projections without the benefit of validation.

Aside from the problems of determining the costs of the war, other shortfalls in accountability resulted in waste and loss of fiscal controls. Millions were spent in direct violation of regulatory restrictions. Units failed to properly record and charge war costs as a Desert Shield/Storm expense, which cost the United States an estimated $126 million in potential reimbursement from our allies.

Once again, not having a deployable financial management capability was front and center. Literally thousands of pay transactions were manually prepared in-theater and shipped back home for processing, resulting in late payments, missing documents, and an overwhelming workload for those at the home station. Also, deploying with a briefcase full of cash and checks proved difficult to manage and secure.

Despite the lessons of Vietnam that highlighted a renewed importance on military pay, those problems were persistent throughout Desert Shield/Storm. The lack of preparedness to process pay and allowances for reservists called to active duty was troubling at best. In fact, 35 percent of all reservists released from active duty after the war left indebted to the government. Support for those already on active duty was equally challenging. Total overpayments in-theater reached a high of nearly $80 million and involved some 120,000 personnel. Additionally, the fact that a large number of individual service members failed to plan their personal financial obligations produced many cases of "bad" checks and overdue creditor accounts.

Having endured the war of my generation, I did not expect to encounter war again. However, when Operations Enduring Freedom and Iraqi Freedom began, I was the major command comptroller for ACC and once again found myself in the throes of wartime financial support. Having spent several years outside the financial management career field, I assumed that the shortfalls I experienced during Operation Desert Shield/Storm had been resolved—they had not.

The hundreds of financial managers who deployed to the Middle East were not prepared for the tasks facing them. Once again, financial troops boarded airplanes with briefcases full of cash and checks. They struggled with check cashing, account balancing, tracking assistance in kind, foreign currency exchanges, and vendor payments. Again, thousands of documents were mailed back to the CONUS for processing, and many of them were either missing or illegible.

To help, assistance visits were provided for on-the-spot training. Eventually, an "emergency" predeployment course was created to provide "just-in-time" training for those deploying to the theater. Despite those herculean efforts, financial management issues persisted throughout the war. Additionally, financial matters such as providing coinage in-theater and managing wartime pay entitlements to avoid inaccuracies with W-2 forms presented new challenges. Following major combat operations, GAO and Air Force auditors highlighted many of those shortfalls.

A GAO audit found that over $100 million had been spent on items that were not needed for the war. This discovery led to a larger issue of a lack of DOD oversight and guidance as to what *should* rather than what *could* be purchased during war. An Air Force audit that discovered guidelines for managing NAFs was totally disregarded. In fact, MWR profits that should have been reinvested in-theater were diverted to fund projects in the CONUS. Finally, the Air Force was singled out for its shortcomings in estimating the costs of the war by identifying instances of both overestimating and underestimating on key wartime tasks.

Having interviewed a number of financial managers with firsthand knowledge of financial performance during the war, I found their conclusions all too familiar. They all agreed that financial training and preparedness were woefully inadequate. They also acknowledged that poor preparedness stemmed from the fact that financial management duties and training during peacetime are nothing like the demands of a war zone.

For me, this open-and-shut case ruled that the comptroller community, which performs so brilliantly during peacetime, was unprepared to perform as effectively during war. This ruling is critical because most experts agree that military excursions in the future will be much more complex. Future conflicts are likely to be more frequent and involve fragile coalition and US public support. Competing domestic priorities will place a premium on financial resources allocated for foreign intervention. Therefore, the financial management of those scarce dollars will undergo even greater scrutiny in the future.

An Opportunity to Change History

Throughout the history of money and war, it is clear that individual military financial managers did not fail—poor DOD business practices and wartime financial training failed. The good news is we can turn the page. The solutions to correcting the failures of financial management during war are well within reach. The current financial paradigm is grounded in peacetime operations. We simply need to reverse our thinking and focus more on being prepared for war. The only quandary is whether we continue on the path of unpreparedness or step up to the challenge and correct the mistakes of the past.

In the future, funds allocated to support military intervention will not only compete with domestic priorities but also endure intense public and congressional oversight. Those conditions place great pressure on DOD military managers to develop systems and training that can withstand the tougher scrutiny. Therefore, we must transform financial wartime procedures and systematically implement those procedures to ensure we are prepared to win the financial "fight" during the next conflict.

According to Proverbs 29:18 (KJV), "Where there is no vision, the people perish." The foundation of a financial wartime transformation must start with a financial vision or concept of operations (CONOPS) that should spell out higher headquarters' oversight responsibilities and be specific enough to guide spending patterns during contingency operations—without overly restricting deployed commanders. The CONOPS should also serve as the universal, authoritative document for contingency financial operations and be periodically updated to ensure current relevance.

We must then tackle the issue of automation support. Many people have suggested that the answer to the financial ills of the past rests with new and faster computers that can operate in austere environments. While I do not necessarily disagree with that assessment, perhaps we should first reexamine the requirements for financial support on the battlefield.

Today, Internet connectivity can provide the support needed to manage most financial transactions between deployed locations and home stations. Deployed members should have the capability to manage their financial transactions in a war zone the same way they manage their personal finances today—online. Routine transactions such as changing allotments or withholding adjustments can and should be accomplished with a desktop or laptop computer or with an application on a cell phone. At a minimum, financial transactions can be accomplished via a telephone call.

We can and should replace pay windows with financial "transaction rooms" at deployed locations. Cashing checks and foreign currency exchanges should be accomplished by using credit or debit cards at ATM machines. Today's technology allows remote-interface access into home-station defense financial systems from anywhere on the planet. Therefore, deployed financial managers can transmit financial data (for example, updating special combat zone entitlements) directly to the home station for immediate posting. Doing so will allow forward financial managers to focus on direct support to their commanders by maintaining budget balances, tracking expenditures, and ensuring that fiscal laws and policies are properly observed. As an added bonus, this action should significantly reduce the footprint of financial managers needed at the deployed location.

I also recommend establishing a contingency finance capability located in the CONUS something akin to a combined air and space operations center. I would name this new capability the contingency financial management operations center (CFMOC), charged with providing 24/7 financial support for deployed forces, including policy guidance on the proper use of appropriated funds. Additionally, just as US fighter pilots "sharpen" their skills by attending predeployment training at Red Flag exercises, so should the CFMOC offer financial predeployment training as required.

The CFMOC can be established through one of two options. The first is simply to assign this duty to the recently established Air Force installation and mission support center. The second is to designate specific billets and a designated location that can be operational within 72 hours of notification. In both options, preoperational training is critical to ensure that personnel assigned to CFMOC duties are trained specifically for war operations—not just in-garrison duties. Also, periodic exercises should be conducted to maintain their operational readiness.

Finally, CFMOC operations should be tested, stressed, and graded during operational inspections.

Neither option requires new manpower billets. However, creation of the CFMOC will demand focused and comprehensive training. To build a sense of pride and camaraderie within the CFMOC, we should consider designating those billets as "combat comptrollers" by adding an Air Force specialty code identifier. To take it a step farther, we should evaluate the pros of adding a special patch or badge to demonstrate to those in the comptroller career field that the CFMOC is an elite assignment, reserved for the best and brightest.

We also need to improve our cost projection and analysis capability. History validates that Congress has been very critical of the DOD's inability to provide accurate cost accounting data and estimates of war costs—and for good reason. As difficult as it is to admit, the accounting system used by the Air Force today, the General Accounting and Financial System (GAFS), was actually installed in 1965! The GAFS does not comply with current general auditing and accounting standards. The good news is the Air Force is in the midst of installing a new auditing/accounting standards compliant system—the Defense Enterprise Accounting Management System (DEAMS). However, it will not be fully implemented until the end of fiscal year 2017.

Even when the DEAMS is operational, we will still need the capability to project war costs. In the past, all Air Force installation comptroller squadrons had a cost-analysis branch with analysts trained in cost estimating. I am very aware of this capability because as an enlisted member and a junior officer, I was one of those analysts. Unfortunately, those cost-estimating branches were eliminated. As a solution, we should reinstate that *capability* as a skill set required for financial managers. That is not to imply we need additional people; rather, we need to train our current financial force in cost-estimating techniques.

If preparedness leads to better war performance, then training leads to better preparedness. Unfortunately, history proves that our deployed financial managers were not prepared. A previous financial/contracting deployment training exercise called Top Dollar, which no longer exists, was an excellent opportunity to hone deployed financial and contracting skills based on the lessons learned from Operation Desert Shield/Storm. I attended several Top Dollar training exercises, and it did indeed provide realistic and intense wartime training. Top Dollar was a huge leap forward in financial war-skills training, and we should bring it back, albeit in a different configuration. Rather than the large footprint of the past, Top Dollar "skills" should be part of every wing comptroller's training program.

For example, during wing exercises, as was the case with Top Dollar, financial and contracting personnel should demonstrate their ability to manage cash, contracts, and foreign currency exchanges in a wartime environment. Wing financial managers should "deploy" locally to a location on the base and be required to demonstrate their ability to conduct financial transactions remotely, both online and manually if necessary. This training should be realistic, rigorous, and tested by major command inspectors general to ensure that future financial performance during war does not mirror past performance.

Additionally, we should take advantage of this opportunity to train the general base populace on personal financial management. Thus, during the exercise deployment phase, random Air Force members should be required to demonstrate their ability to manage personal finances and ensure that family arrangements are in place to continue routine household financial management. Furthermore, we must modernize and streamline the Reserve and Guard pay systems to ensure a smooth transition into and out of contingency deployments. In particular, the total force financial management team should share in wing exercises and hold billets in the CFMOC.

Finally, we should encourage those financial managers with war experience to document and record their experiences and lessons learned. Among other reasons, I decided to publish this monograph because there is very little written about Air Force financial experiences in war. Googling the phrase Army financial management during war will yield countless pages of articles and books. Googling the same information for Air Force produces virtually nothing. We simply must catch up with our Army and Marine Corps financial brethren.

Now that I am retired from the US Air Force, it is certain that I will no longer participate in war. What is not certain is whether or not the Air Force will finally accept and do something about the fact that wartime financial training and preparedness is inadequate. I would like to be optimistic that positive change will happen, but I am not sure. When I inquired about the status of the OIF/OEF financial get-well plan, I could not find anyone who had even heard about either the conference or the report. I found this fact disturbing, but I was not at all surprised. This has been our history. This is why my examination of financial management during war conclusively and consistently showed a lack of training and preparedness. This is precisely why I wrote this monograph. I sincerely hope and pray that the Air Force financial community will take heed of our history during war, lest yet again we watch history repeat itself.

As a final tribute, I would be remiss if I did not acknowledge the extraordinary efforts of financial personnel on the field of battle. Although history does not give financial preparedness during war a flattering score overall, that assessment is no reflection on the hard work and dedicated support of the individual financial managers. Through uncertainty, insufficient training, and inadequate equipment, these personnel have persisted repeatedly during periods of conflict to provide the best fiscal support possible.

Also, through all the problems, it is important to keep in perspective that although there remains much room for improvement, we are much better than whoever claims to be second best! Financial managers indeed have a proud history of achievement during war despite the shortcomings of guidance, training, emphasis, and resources, and I consider myself fortunate to be included among their ranks. Now is the time to capitalize on the lessons from the past and to take the journey of transformation into the future.

Abbreviations

AAFES	Army and Air Force Exchange Service
ACC	Air Combat Command
AF	Air Force
AFA	Air Force Association
AOR	area of responsibility
BAS	basic allowance for subsistence
CCO	contingency contracting officer
CFMA	Centralized Financial Management Agency
CFMOC	contingency financial management operations center
CONOPS	concept of operations
CONUS	continental United States
DEAMS	Defense Enterprise Accounting Management System
DFAS	Defense Finance and Accounting Service
DOD	Department of Defense
GAFS	General Accounting and Financial System
GAO	General Accounting Office (Government Accountability Office)
GPC	government purchase card
ICAF	Industrial College of the Armed Forces
IT	information technology
LES	leave and earnings statement
MACV	Military Assistance Command, Vietnam
MPC	military pay certificate
MRE	meal, ready to eat
MWR	morale, welfare, and recreation
NAF	nonappropriated fund
NCO	noncommissioned officer
O&M	operation and maintenance
OEF	Operation Enduring Freedom

OIF	Operation Iraqi Freedom
PAYSET	pay support evaluation team
PGC	Persian Gulf Command
POW	prisoner of war
R&R	rest and recuperation
SWPA	Southwest Pacific area
USAFCENT	US Air Forces Central Command
USAFFE	United States Army Forces in the Far East
USCENTAF	United States Central Air Forces
USCENTCOM	United States Central Command

Bibliography

Abbott, Alfred A. "The Army as Banker." *Army Information Digest* 2, no. 8 (August 1947): 37.

Air Force Audit Agency Report, F2010-0001-FD4000. *United States Air Forces Central Area of Responsibility Services Financial Activities.* Washington, DC: USAF, 7 October 2009.

Blomgren, Holton E. "Comptrollership in Vietnam." *Army Finance Journal* (March–April 1967): 12–19.

Brassem, Jan W. "The 'Money' Man in Vietnam." *Air Force Comptroller* 1, no. 1 (October 1967).

Comptroller of the Army. To the Chief of Staff. Memorandum. Subject: Improvement of Accounting Operations in Vietnam and Elsewhere in the U.S. Army, 15 December 1967.

Defense Finance and Accounting Service. "Desert Shield–Desert Storm Servicemembers' Indebtedness." 19 December 1991.

———. "Pay Support Evaluation Team (PAYSET) Concept of Operations." Interoffice memorandum, 25 April 1991.

de Gruchy, Col Oliver Williams, chief, Fiscal Branch, HQ Persian Gulf Command (PGC). To Command Signal Officer, PGSC. Memorandum. 18 January 1943.

Department of Defense Instruction 7720.6. *Cost Reduction Program Reporting System*, 20 January 1964.

DeWitt, Harry M. *Comptrollership in the Armed Forces: A Summary and Comparative Evaluation of Comptrollership in Industry and the Department of Defense with Special Reference to Program Management and Management Engineering as Included in the Functions of the Army Comptroller.* Washington, DC: Institute of Engineering, 1952.

Drea, Edward J. *McNamara, Clifford, and the Burdens of Vietnam, 1965–1969.* Vol. 6. Secretaries of Defense Historical Series. Washington, DC: Historical Office of the Secretary of Defense, 2011.

Fippen, John W. "Combat Support and the Comptroller." *Air Force Comptroller* 2, no. 1 (October 1968): 2–5.

General Accounting Office (GAO). *Defense Budget: Need to Strengthen Guidance and Oversight of Contingency Operations Costs.* GAO-02-450. Washington, DC: GAO, May 2002. http://www.gao.gov/assets/240/234701.pdf.

———. *Operation Desert Shield, Problems Encountered by Activated Reservists.* Report GAO/NSIAD-91-290. Washington, DC: GAO, September 1991.

———. *Report to Congressional Requesters: Contingency Operations, DOD's Reported Costs Contain Significant Inaccuracies.* GAO/NSI AD-96-115 Washington, DC: GAO, May 1996, http://www.gao.gov/assets/160/155431.pdf.

Headquarters, United States Military Assistance Command, Vietnam. Chief of Staff Action Memorandum No. 70-44. MACCO-F. Subject: Conservation of MACV Resources, 8 April 1970.

Hershey, William. "War's Cost Cannot Be Calculated." *Philadelphia Inquirer*, 24 January 1991. http://articles.philly.com/1991-01-24/news/25819990_1_war-ends-war-cost-korean-war.

Hewes, James E. *From Root to McNamara: Army Organization and Administration, 1900–1963.* Washington, DC: Center of Military History, 1975.

House. *Congressional Record* 89. 78th Cong., 1st sess., 1943.

———. *Hearing before the Committee on the Budget.* 102nd Cong., 1st sess., 1991.

———. *National Defense Authorization Act for Fiscal Years 1992 and 1993.* Conference Report to Accompany HR 2100, report 102–311.

———. *Report of the Committee on Appropriations on Department of Defense Appropriations Bill, 2003.* 107th Cong., 2nd sess., 2002. https://www.congress.gov/107/crpt/hrpt532/CRPT-107hrpt532.pdf.

Joint Logistics Review Board. *Logistics Support in the Vietnam Era.* Washington, DC: Department of Defense, 1970.

Joint Universal Lessons Learned (JULLS). Report 62163-79755, *Centralized Funding of Contingency Operations*, 26 June 1991.

Kaplan, Fred. "White House Refuses to Disclose Desert Shield Costs to Congress." *Boston Globe*, 7 January 1991.

Maddox, Col L. W., chief financial officer, SWPA. To FIS DIR, ASF. Letter. Subject: Progress Report of Fiscal and Finance Activities in SWPA, 8 December 1943.

Message. Department of the Army. DA 818750. Subject: *Services and Supplies Provided Others*, 9 June 1967.

Message. Headquarters, United States Army, Pacific. GPCO 26099. 1 August 1967.

Military Intelligence Section, Far East Command. *History of the United States Army Forces in the Far East, 1943–1945*. Manila, Philippines: US Army, 1974.

Morgan, Gregory L. "Comptroller Warplanning Implementation Plan: Detailed Outline." Working draft. Headquarters USAF, 30 March 2002.

"Most Desert Storm Reservists Experienced Pay Problems." *Army Reserve Magazine*, no. 4. 1991.

Nelson, Soraya S. "We Were Just Forgotten, Doctors Say Desert Storm Wrecked Them Financially." *Air Force Times*, 18 October 1993.

Odell, Col R. E., fiscal director, HQ United States Army Forces in the Middle East (USAFIME). For CG, USAFIME. Memorandum. Subj: Report of Operations. 22 December 44.

Office of the Assistant Secretary of the Air Force (Financial Management). "Financial Management and Comptroller Desert Shield/Storm Lessons Learned Action Items." Memorandum. 13 August 1991.

Office of the Secretary of the Air Force (Financial Management). "Financial Management and Comptroller Desert Shield/Storm Lessons Learned Action Items." Memorandum. 13 August 1991.

Ostrander, Brig Gen L. S., adjutant general, USAFFE. To TAG. Letter. Subj: Discontinuance of Class E Allotments 6. September 1943.

Pay Support Evaluation Team (PAYSET), United States Army. *Military Pay Support to the Army, Operations DESERT SHIELD/ STORM, August 1990–June 1991*. Washington, DC: DOD, 1991. http://www.dtic.mil/dtic/tr/fulltext/u2/a251327.pdf.

Power, Kevin. "Financial Systems Can't Track War Costs Accurately." *Government Computer News*. 4 February 1991.

Riley, Karen. "1st Day of Desert Storm Cost at Least $500 Million." *Washington Times*. 18 January 1991.

Rundell, Walter Jr. *Black Market Money: Collapse of U.S. Military Currency Control in World War II*. Baton Rouge: Louisiana State University Press, 1964.

———. *Military Money: A Fiscal History of the U.S. Army Overseas in World War II*. College Station: Texas A&M University Press, 1980.

Sasser, Jim. "Is Uncle Sam Getting Stiffed?" *New York Times*. 19 December 1990.

SecDef. For Service Secretaries and JCS. Memorandum. 1 March 1965. Folder: Official Correspondence: Army Chief of Staff, Close Hold, Box 76. H. K. Johnson Papers. Military History Institute.

Seelig, Louis C. *Resource Management in Peace and War*. Washington, DC: National Defense University Press, 1990.

Senate. *Hearing before the Committee on Armed Services: "Lessons Learned" During Operation Enduring Freedom in Afghanistan and Operation Iraqi Freedom, and Ongoing Operations in the United States Central Command Region*. 108th Cong., 1st sess. 9 July 2003. https://www.gpo.gov/fdsys/pkg/CHRG-108shrg96501 /html/CHRG-108shrg96501.htm.

"'Shock and Awe' Campaign underway in Iraq." *CNN Student News*. 22 March 2003. http://edition.cnn.com/2003/fyi/news/03/22/iraq.war.

Task Force Enduring Look, United States Air Force. *Air Force Performance in Desert Storm*. Washington, DC: DOD, April 1991. http://www.dtic.mil/dtic/tr/fulltext/u2/a235941.pdf.

Taylor, Leonard B. *Financial Management of the Vietnam Conflict: 1962–1972*. Washington, DC: GPO, 1974.

Tucker, Spencer. *Encyclopedia of the Vietnam War: A Political, Social, and Military History*. Santa Barbara, CA: ABC-CLIO, 1998.

Wines, Michael. "After the War: P.O.W.'S; Ex-P.O.W.'S Offer Accounts of Terror and Torture in Iraq." *New York Times*. 15 March 1991. http://www.nytimes.com/1991/03/15/world/after-the-war-pow -s-ex-pow-s-offer-accounts-of-terror-and-torture-in-iraq.html.